MW01670551

800
Ninja Foodi
Cookbook

Easy and Delicious Recipes for Your Ninja Foodi
Multi-Cooker

By Linda Michael

Copyright ©2020 By Linda Michael
All rights reserved.

No part of this guide may be reproduced in any form without permission in writing from the publisher except in the case of brief quotations embodied in critical articles or reviews.

Legal & Disclaimer

The information contained in this book and its contents is not designed to replace or take the place of any form of medical or professional advice; and is not meant to replace the need for independent medical, financial, legal or other professional advice or services, as may be required. The content and information in this book has been provided for educational and entertainment purposes only.

The content and information contained in this book has been compiled from sources deemed reliable, and it is accurate to the best of the Author's knowledge, information and belief. However, the Author cannot guarantee its accuracy and validity and cannot be held liable for any errors and/or omissions. Further, changes are periodically made to this book as and when needed. Where appropriate and/or necessary, you must consult a professional (including but not limited to your doctor, attorney, financial advisor or such other professional advisor) before using any of the suggested remedies, techniques, or information in this book.

Upon using the contents and information contained in this book, you agree to hold harmless the Author from and against any damages, costs, and expenses, including any legal fees potentially resulting from the application of any of the information provided by this book. This disclaimer applies to any loss, damages or injury caused by the use and application, whether directly or indirectly, of any advice or information presented, whether for breach of contract, tort, negligence, personal injury, criminal intent, or under any other cause of action.

Table of content

Introduction

Ninja Foodi delivers a whole new way of cooking by providing a super combination of power, speed, and technology. It offers wholesome meals with great texture and flavor prepared from real foods. It's time to stop settling for convenience with delicious meals.

Pressure cooking has been in practice for decades; we all are fond of our grandma's favorite recipes that have been invented using classic stovetop pressure cookers. Ninja Foodi multi-cookers and pressure cookers are just the same but with advanced features for ease of cooking.

Ninja Foodi is also popularly known as "one-pot wonder" for providing multiple cooking functions to cook a wide range of foods without using any additional unit but its core cooking pot.

- **Multi-cookers**

Multi-cookers models are available in 8-quarts and 6.5-quarts. Being a multi-cooker, it combines two functions of pressure cooking and Air Crisp technology for air frying. It acts as both a pressure cooker and an air fryer as it comes with two lids (Pressure Lid and Crisping Lid). Moreover, it also acts as a slow-cooker with slow cooking function.

- **Pressure Cooking**

Ninja Foodi pressure cookers include all the features and functions of multi-cooker except Air Crisp technology. Pressure cooker models are available in 8-quarts, 6.5-quarts, and 5-quartz.

It allows you to cook all types of pressure cooking and slow cooking cuisines. It comes with only Pressure Lid. However, some advanced models are offering

- **Air Frying & Crisping**

Air Fryers are, as the name suggests, for preparing crispy foods using Air Crisp technology. It comes with only Crisping Lid.

Chapter 1 The Basics of Ninja Foodi Pressure Cooker

Cooking Parts & Features

Ninja Foodi provides a range of parts and features for a totally safe and convenient cooking experience.

Cooking Pot

- Main pot to add all cooking ingredients; this pot is connected to a central heating unit that generated high-pressure steam while cooking to tenderize inside the food. With this cooking pot, you can also do open-lid cooking such as sautéing and meat browning.

Pressure Lid

- Pressure lid is for typical pressure cooking. After closing the pressure lid over the cooking pot, it creates an air-tight locked chamber that holds high-pressure steam to tenderize inside the food.

Crisping Lid

- Crisping lid is the lid for preparing all types of snacks and crispy foods such as chicken tenders, French fries, chips, and so on. To make it, you have to use this lid and select the "Air Crisp" mode.

Also, many recipes call for the session of initial pressure cooking followed by the session of crisping to nicely caramelized meals; crisping lid enables you to add that crispiness to your meals.

Pressure Release Valve

- This valve enables the locking of inside pressure and release of pressure after cooking is completed. This valve needs to be kept in a LOCKED position to pressure cook foods and needs to be held in the VENT position to release build up steam.

Reversible Rack

- Reversible rack does the usual function to serve as a platform to place a baking pan or food directly over it. It prevents foods from touching the surface of the cooking pot. For example, foods such as vegetables, fish, shrimp, etc.

can be put directly over it (either raw or after seasoning) to tenderize using high-pressure steam.

You can reverse it and use it to broil foods. For that, you have to select the "BROIL" function and set the desired temperature level.

Crisping Basket

- Crisping basket is usually of 4-quart size with ceramic coating. As the name suggests, it is used to prepare crispy snacks such as French fries, crispy nuggets, crunchy chicken wings, chips, roasted nuts, and so on. It cooks foods over the "AIR CRISP" cooking function.

Other Parts

Additional parts include a floating valve, silicon ring, air outlet vent, anti-clog cap, heat shield, and control panel.

Separate Accessories

Based on your cooking requirements, Ninja Foodi offers additional accessories that need to be purchased separately. These accessories include loaf pan, multi-purpose baking pan, roasting rack insert, crisper pan, and dehydrating rack.

Control Panel

The control panel is equipped with multiple custom cooking features to make cooking a fun experience for you.

PRESSURE – The most commonly used function to tenderize ingredients using high-pressure steam.

STEAM – Use this function to steam foods at high temperatures.

SEAR/SAUTE – For open-lid sautéing common cooking ingredients and simmering sauces without closing the cooking pot.

SLOW COOK – Slow cooking is another way of preparing foods, which are usually 4 hours to 10 hours of cooking time.

AIR CRISP – To prepare crispy foods and snacks.

BAKE/ROAST – Using this function, you can prepare baked recipes and tender meats.

GRILL – Mostly used to prepare grilled foods for caramelizing and browning.

TEMPERATURE ADJUSTMENT - Use Up and Down buttons to adjust temperature.

START/STOP - To initiate the cooking process or stop cooking in between.

KEEP WARM - After the recipe is done the cooking, you can opt to keep it warm until ready to serve. You can keep it warm for up to 12 hours by just adjusting the time of your choice. However, this function is not for warming up cold or frozen foods. It is recommended to thaw frozen foods, discard liquid, and add them in the pot to cook.

STAND BY – If you left the unit unattended after cooking time is over, it automatically goes into standby mode after 10 minutes.

QUICK PRESSURE RELEASE – If your recipe calls for quick pressure release, you can set the pressure valve to the VENT position right after cooking time is over. It quickly released build up pressure; some steam might remain inside, which will escape after you open the top lid.

NATURAL PRESSURE RELEASE – If your recipe calls for natural pressure release, it requires pressure to release in its natural way. After cooking time gets over, Ninja Foodi starts releasing inside pressure automatically for 8-10 minutes in a gradual manner. During this time frame, it will automatically switch to the KEEP WARM function. Then after, you can choose to set the pressure valve to the VENT position to release the remaining pressure.

What Makes Ninja Foodi So Popular

The popularity of Ninja Foodi can be certainly justified given its ease of use powered by advanced safety features and technologically advanced cooking functions. Let's take a peek on why Ninja Foodi is the best investment to resolve all your cooking blues.

One-Pot Cooking

Sauté onions and garlic, pressure cook meats, grains, and vegetables followed by air crisping using the same pot. From sautéing, pressure cooking, slow cooking, baking, roasting to broiling, you need one pot to accomplish all cooking tasks.

Nutritious Meals in Quick Time

As compared to traditional cooking methods, Ninja Foodi cooks meals in 70% less time without compromising on taste and nutrition. It takes less cooking liquid to tenderize vegetables, meat cuts, fish, and seafood ingredients. By utilizing almost all liquid, essential nutrients remain intact within the meals instead of being washed away in left-over liquid.

Wholesome Meals Just As You Like

Cooking pot of this fantastic appliance allows you to cook foods in parts to enjoy their natural texture. For instance, grains and vegetables need more time to tenderize than delicate meat cuts. This is where Ninja Foodi can allow you to customize your cooking for the best results. You can cook grains with some veggies to start with and then later add your favorite meat cuts and continue cooking until each ingredient is ideally tenderized. That way, you can ensure that each ingredient maintains its ideal texture with the ideal nutrient ratio.

Crisp Meals

Stove-top cookers use high pressure and high-temperature steam to tenderize added foods. Ninja Foodi goes beyond that by providing a crisping option. Multi-cooker and air frying models come with the Crisping Lid. You can use a pressure lid to tenderize your foods first, and then, for the same meal, you can use the Crisping Lid for cooking caramelized and perfectly crisped meals. That way, you can enjoy meals that are crisp on the outside and tender inside.

Safe Cooking

Ninja Foodi uses extremely high pressure steam to food in minutes; however, it also ensures total safety as all models come with 14 pre-tested safety features for worry-free cooking and peace of mind.

One-Pot Cleaning

Yes, you only have one pot to clean after cooking is done. No more pile of utensils to clean that takes almost the same time as cooking. Not to mention, cleaning feels the most boring task to do after you are done with cooking. With minimal clean ups required, you can take a sigh of relief as your post-cooking tasks are negligible.

The cooking pot is nonstick, ceramic coated, and is dishwasher safe to make cleaning a breeze for you.

Chapter2 Breakfast Recipes

Sausage Rolls

Prep + Cooking Time: 18 minutes, Servings: 4

Ingredients:

- 8 pork sausages
- 8 crescent roll dough pieces
- 8 cheddar cheese slices

Directions:

1. Unroll the crescent roll pieces on a working surface, divide sausages and the cheese on them, roll and seal the edges. Place the rolls in the Foodi's basket and cook on Roast mode at 400 °F for 8 minutes. Serve the rolls for breakfast

Basil Omelet

Prep + Cooking Time: 15 minutes, Servings: 4

Ingredients:

- 4 eggs; whisked.
- 1 cup buttermilk
- 1 tbsp. basil; chopped.
- 2 tbsp. butter, soft
- A pinch of salt and black pepper

Directions:

1. In a bowl mix all the ingredients except the butter and whisk well. Grease the Foodi's baking pan with the butter and pour the basil omelet mix inside
2. Put the reversible rack in the machine, add the baking pan and cook the omelet on Baking mode at 400 °F for 10 minutes. Divide the omelet between plates and serve for breakfast

Greek Potato

Prep + Cooking Time: 25 minutes, Servings: 4

Ingredients:

- 4 oz. Greek yogurt
- 1 ½ lbs. gold potatoes; cubed.
- 1 tbsp. sweet paprika
- 1 tbsp. cilantro; chopped.
- 2 tbsp. olive oil
- Salt and black pepper to the taste

Directions:

1. Set the Foodi on Sauté mode, add the oil, heat it up, add the potatoes and cook for 5 minutes. Add the paprika, cilantro, salt and pepper, set the machine on Air Crisp and cook for 15 minutes at 350 °F
2. Divide the potatoes into bowls, add the yogurt on top, toss a bit and serve for breakfast

Sausage Pockets

Prep + Cooking Time: 40 minutes, Servings: 4

Ingredients:

- 6 oz. sausage, ground
- 2 puff pastry sheets, each cut in 4 rectangles
- 1 cup cheddar cheese, shredded
- 2 eggs; whisked.
- A pinch of salt and black pepper
- 2 tbsp. olive oil

Directions:

1. Place the sausage in the Foodi's basket, set the machine on Roast and cook at 375 °F for 15 minutes. Add the eggs, salt and pepper to the basket, cook for 5 more minutes and transfer everything to a plate
2. Divide this mix on 4 rectangles of puff pastry, sprinkle the cheese, top with the other puff pastry pieces, seal edges and brush the pockets with the oil
3. Place the baking pan in the Foodi, add the pockets, set the pot on Air Fry and cook at 400 °F for 6 minutes more. Divide the pockets between plates and serve

Brown Sugar Oatmeal

Prep + Cooking Time: 25 minutes, Servings: 4

Ingredients:

- 1 cup steel cut oats
- 1 cup milk
- 2 and ½ cups water
- 2 tsp. vanilla extract
- 2 tbsp. brown sugar

Directions:

1. Put all the ingredients in the Foodi, seal with the pressure lid and cook on High for 15 minutes. Release the pressure naturally for 10 minutes, divide the oatmeal into bowls and serve for breakfast

Coconut Bowls

Prep + Cooking Time: 20 minutes, Servings: 2

Ingredients:

- 2 bananas, peeled and sliced
- 1 ½ tbsp. cocoa powder
- 1 cup almond milk
- 4 tbsp. coconut, shredded
- 2 tbsp. almond butter
- ¼ tsp. vanilla extract

Directions:

1. Put the reversible rack in the Foodi and place the baking pan inside
2. Put all the ingredients in the pan, set the machine on Bake mode and cook at 300 °F for 10 minutes. Divide into 2 bowls and serve for breakfast

Breakfast Gold Potatoes And Bacon

Prep + Cooking Time: 50 minutes, Servings: 8

Ingredients:

- 8 oz. bacon; chopped.
- 2 gold potatoes; cubed.
- 4 eggs; whisked.
- 1 yellow onion; chopped.
- 1 red bell pepper; chopped.
- A pinch of salt and black pepper
- 1 tsp. sweet paprika

Directions:

1. Set the Foodi on Sauté mode, add the bacon and cook it for 4-5 minutes. Add the onion, bell pepper and potatoes, toss and sauté for 5 more minutes
2. Add salt, pepper, the paprika and the eggs, set the Foodi on Air Crisp mode and cook for 30 minutes at 360 °F, shaking the machine halfway. Divide everything between plates and serve

Polenta Balls

Prep + Cooking Time: 25 minutes, Servings: 4

Ingredients:

- 1 cup cornmeal
- 3 cups water
- ¼ cup cornstarch
- A drizzle of olive oil
- 1 tbsp. butter, soft
- Salt to taste

Directions:

1. Put the water in a pot, heat up over medium heat, add the cornmeal and salt, whisk and cook for 10 minutes. Add the butter, whisk well, take off the heat and cool down
2. Take spoon fools of polenta, shape balls and dredge them in cornstarch
3. Place the balls in the Foodi's basket and cook on Air Crisp for 15 minutes at 360 °F, shaking the machine halfway. Divide between plates and serve for breakfast.

Oatmeal Casserole

Prep + Cooking Time: 30 minutes, Servings: 6

Ingredients:

- 1 banana, peeled and mashed
- 2 cups milk
- 2 eggs; whisked.
- 2 cups old fashioned oats
- 1/3 cup sugar
- 1 cup blueberries
- 2 tbsp. butter
- 1 tsp. cinnamon powder
- 1 tsp. baking powder
- 1 tsp. vanilla extract
- Cooking spray

Directions:

1. In a bowl mix the sugar with baking powder, cinnamon, blueberries, banana, milk, eggs, butter, vanilla and whisk. Grease the Foodi's baking dish with cooking spray, add oats on the bottom, add the berries and banana mix and toss
2. Put the reversible rack in the machines, put the baking dish inside, put the pressure lid on, seal and cook on High for 20 minutes. Release the pressure naturally for 10 minutes, divide into bowls and serve for breakfast.

Tomato Toast

Prep + Cooking Time: 11 minutes, Servings: 3

Ingredients:

- 6 bread slices
- 3 garlic cloves; minced.
- 1 cup mozzarella cheese; grated.
- 5 tbsp. butter, melted
- 6 tsp. tomato pesto

Directions:

1. Arrange bread slices on a working surface, spread the butter and all the other ingredients on each.
2. Add the basket in the Foodi machine, add the bread slices inside, set the pot on Air Crisp and cook everything for 8 minutes at 350 °F. Divide the toast between plates and serve

Delicious Frittata

Prep + Cooking Time: 35 minutes, Servings: 6

Ingredients:

- 8 oz. white mushrooms, sliced
- 2 leeks; chopped.
- 12 eggs; whisked.
- ½ cup crème fraiche
- 1 cup cheddar cheese, shredded
-
- 1 cup water
- 3 tbsp. olive oil
- 2 tbsp. parsley; chopped.
- A pinch of salt and black pepper

Directions:

1. Set the Foodi on Sauté mode, add the oil and heat it up. Add the leeks, stir and cook for 5 minutes. Add the mushrooms, stir and cook for another 5 minutes
2. In a bowl mix the eggs with the crème fraiche, parsley, salt and pepper and whisk. Add the sautéed mushrooms mix and stir again
3. Add the water to the Foodi, add the reversible rack, add the baking pan inside and pour the eggs mixture inside
4. Set the Foodi on High Pressure and cook everything for 10 minutes. Release the pressure fast for 5 minutes, divide the frittata between plates and serve

Mexican Breakfast

Prep + Cooking Time: 20 minutes, Servings: 2

Ingredients:

- 1 green bell pepper, sliced
- 2 eggs; whisked.
- 1 avocado, peeled, pitted and sliced
- 2 tortillas
- 2 tbsp. cheddar cheese; grated.
- 2 tbsp. salsa
- Salt and black pepper to the taste

Directions:

1. In a bowl mix all the ingredients except the tortillas and toss them. Put all the ingredients in the Foodi, put the pressure lid on, seal and cook on High for 10 minutes, shaking the Foodi halfway
2. Release the pressure naturally for 10 minutes, divide the bell peppers mix on the tortillas, roll them and serve for breakfast

Breakfast Hasbrown Casserole

Prep + Cooking Time: 40 minutes, Servings: 10

Ingredients:

- 1 lb. ham; chopped.
- 48 oz. hashbrowns
- ½ cup cheddar cheese, shredded
- 1 yellow onion; chopped.
- ¼ cup milk
- 6 eggs; whisked.
- 3 tbsp. olive oil

Directions:

1. Set your Foodi on sauté mode, add the oil, heat it up, add the onion, stir and cook for 3-4 minutes.
2. Add hashbrowns and the ham, set the Foodi on Air Crisp and cook for 15 minutes, stirring everything halfway
3. Add eggs mixed with hashbrowns and cook everything on Air Crisp for 10 minutes more. Sprinkle the cheese on top, divide everything between plates and serve for breakfast

Bacon And Mushrooms

Prep + Cooking Time: 17 minutes, Servings: 4

Ingredients:

- 10 brown mushrooms, sliced
- ½ cup heavy cream
- ¼ cup cheddar cheese; grated.
- 3 eggs; whisked.
- 1 red onion; chopped.
- 1 tbsp. canola oil
- 2 tbsp. bacon; chopped.
- ½ tsp. thyme, dried
- Salt and black pepper to the taste

Directions:

1. Set the Foodi on Sauté mode, add the oil and heat it up. Add the bacon, stir and cook for 3 minutes. Add the onion, thyme and the mushrooms, stir and sauté for 4 more minutes
2. Add the eggs mixed with the cream, salt and pepper, set the Foodi on Air Crisp and cook everything for 8 minutes at 370 °F. Sprinkle the cheese all over, toss the mix a bit, divide between plates and serve for breakfast

Cheese Peppers Frittata

Prep + Cooking Time: 30 minutes, Servings: 6

Ingredients:

- 6 oz. jarred roasted red bell peppers; chopped.
- 3 garlic cloves; minced.
- 12 eggs; whisked.
- ½ cup parmesan; grated.
- 2 tbsp. parsley; chopped.
- 2 tbsp. chives; chopped.
- 6 tbsp. ricotta cheese
- A drizzle of olive oil
- Salt and black pepper to the taste

Directions:

1. In a bowl mix the bell peppers with the eggs, garlic, parsley, salt, pepper, chives and ricotta and whisk. Grease the Foodi's baking pan with the oil and pour the eggs mixture inside
2. Add the reversible rack to the machine, add the baking pan and cook on Baking mode at 300 °F for 20 minutes. Divide between plates and serve

Ninja Baked Omelet

Prep + Cooking Time: 40 minutes, Servings: 6

Ingredients:

- ½ cup red bell pepper; chopped.
- ½ cup green bell pepper; chopped.
- ½ cup chives; chopped.
- 1 cup ham, cooked and chopped
- 1 cup cheddar cheese, shredded
- ½ cup milk
- 8 eggs; whisked.
- A pinch of salt and black pepper
- Cooking spray

Directions:

1. Put the reversible rack in the Foodi, place the baking pan inside and grease it with cooking spray. In a bowl mix the milk with the eggs, cheese, ham, salt, pepper, bell peppers and the chives and whisk well
2. Pour this into the baking pan, set the Foodi on Bake mode at 315 °F and cook for 30 minutes. Divide the omelet between plates and serve

Paprika Scrambled Eggs

Prep + Cooking Time: 20 minutes, Servings: 4

Ingredients:

- 4 eggs; whisked.
- 1 red onion; chopped.
- A drizzle of olive oil
- 2 tsp. sweet paprika
- Salt and black pepper to the taste

Directions:

1. In a bowl mix the eggs with salt, pepper, the onion and the paprika and whisk. Set the Foodi on Sauté mode, add the oil, heat it up and add the eggs mix
2. Stir everything well, set the Foodi on Air Crisp and cook the eggs for 10 minutes at 360 °F, shaking the machine halfway. Divide between plates and serve for breakfast

Bread And Corn Pudding

Prep + Cooking Time: 55 minutes, Servings: 6

Ingredients:

- 4 bacon slices, cooked and chopped
- 1 ½ cups coconut milk
- 4 eggs; whisked.
- 3 cups bread; cubed.
- 1 tbsp. olive oil
- ½ cup coconut cream
- 2 cups corn
- ½ cup green bell pepper; chopped.
- 1 yellow onion; chopped.
- 3 tbsp. parmesan cheese; grated.
- 1 tsp. thyme; chopped.
- 2 tsp. garlic; grated.
- Salt and black pepper

Directions:

1. Set the Foodi on Sauté mode, add the oil, heat it up, add the onion and garlic, stir and sauté for 5 minutes. Add the corn, bell peppers, thyme, salt and pepper, toss, cook for 5 more minutes and transfer everything to the Foodi's baking pan
2. Add the eggs mixed with the cream, bread and milk and toss everything
3. Place the reversible rack in the machine, add the baking pan inside, sprinkle the parmesan and the bacon on top and cook on Baking mode at 350 °F for 35 minutes. Divide between plates and serve for breakfast.

Cheesy Omelet

Prep + Cooking Time: 15 minutes, Servings: 2

Ingredients:

- 4 eggs; whisked.
- 1 cup cheddar cheese; grated.
- 4 tsp. butter, melted
-
- 1 tbsp. chives; chopped.
- A pinch of salt and black pepper

Directions:

1. In a bowl mix half of the butter with all the other ingredients and whisk. Put the reversible rack in the Foodi, add the baking pan inside and grease it with the remaining butter
2. Add the eggs mix in the pan and cook on Baking mode at 370 °F for 10 minutes. Serve for breakfast

Blackberries Bowls

Prep + Cooking Time: 15 minutes, Servings: 4

Ingredients:

- 1 ½ cups corn flakes
- ¼ cup blackberries
- 3 cups milk
- 2 eggs; whisked.
- 4 tbsp. cream cheese, whipped
- 1 tbsp. sugar
- ¼ tsp. nutmeg, ground

Directions:

1. In a bowl combine all the ingredients, toss them and pour the whole mixture in the Foodi's baking pan.
2. Add the reversible rack in the machine, add the baking pan and cook the mix on Baking mode at 350 °F for 10 minutes. Divide between plates and serve for breakfast

Parmesan Scrambled Eggs

Prep + Cooking Time: 17 minutes, Servings: 4

Ingredients:

- 3 oz. almond milk
- 2 oz. parmesan cheese; grated.
- 4 eggs; whisked.
- A drizzle olive oil
- A splash of Worcestershire sauce

Directions:

1. In a bowl mix all the ingredients except the oil and toss well. Set the Foodi on sauté mode, add the oil, heat it up, add the eggs mix, toss, set the machine on Air Crisp and cook for 12 minutes at 360 °F, shaking the pot from time to time. Divide the eggs between plates and serve for breakfast.

Pear And Walnuts Oatmeal

Prep + Cooking Time: 25 minutes, Servings: 4

Ingredients:

- 2 cups pears, peeled and cubed
- ¼ cups sugar
- 1 cup almond milk
- 1 cup old fashioned oats
- ½ cup walnuts; chopped.
- 1 tbsp. butter, soft
- ½ tsp. cinnamon powder

Directions:

1. Put all the ingredients in the Foodi, toss them, put the pressure lid on and cook on High for 15 minutes. Release the pressure naturally for 10 minutes, divide the oatmeal into bowls and serve for breakfast

Tomato Omelet

Prep + Cooking Time: 40 minutes, Servings: 2

Ingredients:

- 2 eggs; whisked.
- ¼ cup coconut milk
- ½ cup tomatoes; cubed.
- ½ cup cheddar cheese, shredded
- 2 tbsp. spring onions; chopped.
- A pinch of salt and black pepper

Directions:

1. In a bowl mix all the ingredients, toss and pour everything into the Foodi's baking pan
2. Place the reversible rack in the machine, add the baking pan and cook the omelet on Baking mode at 360 °F for 30 minutes. Divide the omelet between plates and serve

Kale Scramble

Prep + Cooking Time: 15 minutes, Servings: 2

Ingredients:

- 2 cups kale, torn
- 2 eggs; whisked.
- 1 small shallot; chopped.
- 1 ½ tbsp. mayonnaise
- 1 tsp. olive oil
- A pinch of salt and black pepper

Directions:

1. Set the Foodi on Sauté mode, add the oil and heat it up. Add the shallot, salt and pepper, stir and cook for 2-3 minutes. Add the kale, toss and cook for 3 more minutes
2. Add the eggs mixed with the mayo, toss everything, set the Foodi on Air Crisp and cook the scramble for 3 minutes at 370 °F. Divide between plates and serve for breakfast

Thyme Omelet

Prep + Cooking Time: 18 minutes, Servings: 6

Ingredients:

- 6 eggs; whisked.
- 1 tsp. thyme, dried
- 2 tbsp. olive oil
- Salt and black pepper to the taste

Directions:

1. Set the Foodi on Sauté mode, add the oil, heat it, up, add the eggs mixed with thyme, salt and pepper, spread into the Foodi, put the pressure lid on and cook on High for 8 minutes. Release the pressure naturally for 10 minutes, divide between plates and serve for breakfast

Chicken Sausage Omelet

Prep + Cooking Time: 20 minutes, Servings: 4

Ingredients:

- 1 chicken sausage link, sliced
- 4 cherry tomatoes; cubed.
- 4 eggs; whisked.
- 1 tbsp. olive oil
- 1 tbsp. cheddar; grated.
- 1 tbsp. parsley; chopped.
- Salt and black pepper to the taste

Directions:

1. Put the sausage in the Foodi's basket, set the machine on Roast, cook at 360 °F for 5 minutes and transfer to the machine's baking pan
2. In a bowl mix all the other ingredients, toss and pour over the sausage. Place the reversible rack in the Foodi, add the baking pan inside and cook everything on Baking mode at 360 °F for 10 minutes. Serve for breakfast.

Almond Hash Browns

Prep + Cooking Time: 30 minutes, Servings: 6

Ingredients:

- 1 ½ lbs. hash browns
- 6 bacon slices; chopped.
- 9 oz. cream cheese
- 1 yellow onion; chopped.
- 1 cup almond milk
- A drizzle of olive oil
- 6 eggs
- 6 spring onions; chopped.
- 2 tbsp. cheddar cheese, shredded
- Salt and black pepper to the taste

Directions:

1. Set your Foodi on sauté mode, add the oil, heat it up, add the onion and spring onions, stir and cook for 5 minutes.
2. Add hash browns and the bacon, set the Foodi on Air Crisp and cook for 15 minutes, stirring everything halfway
3. Add eggs mixed with cream cheese, milk, salt and pepper, toss and cook everything on Air Crisp for 10 minutes more. Divide between plates, sprinkle the cheese on top and serve for breakfast

Quick Apple Oatmeal

Prep + Cooking Time: 25 minutes, Servings: 8

Ingredients:

- 4 apples, cored and cubed
- ½ cup raisins
- 1/3 cup brown sugar
- 2 cups steel cut oats
- 6 cups water
- 2 tbsp. maple syrup
- 1 tbsp. butter
- 1 tsp. cinnamon powder

Directions:

1. Put all the ingredients in the Foodi and toss them. Put the pressure lid on, seal and cook on High for 15 minutes, shaking the Foodi halfway
2. Release the pressure naturally for 10 minutes, stir the oatmeal again, divide into bowls and serve

Creamy Chili

Prep + Cooking Time: 15 minutes, Servings: 4

Ingredients:

- 4 eggs; whisked.
- 1 red chili pepper; chopped.
- 2 tbsp. heavy cream
- 2 tbsp. parsley, finely chopped
- Salt and white pepper to the taste

Directions:

1. In a bowl mix all the ingredients and toss them. Add the reversible rack to the Foodi, add the baking pan and pour the creamy chili mix inside
2. Cook the mix on Baking mode at 400 °F for 10 minutes. Divide the mix between plates and serve

Eggplant Breakfast

Prep + Cooking Time: 40 minutes, Servings: 2

Ingredients:

- 2 eggplants; cubed.
- ¾ cup tomato paste
- 2 cups mozzarella cheese; grated.
- 1 tbsp. avocado oil
- 2 tbsp. cheddar; grated.
- 2 tbsp. fresh basil; chopped.
- 2 tbsp. coconut milk
- ½ tsp. garlic powder
- 2 tsp. cilantro; chopped.
- ½ tsp. Italian seasoning
- Salt and black pepper to the taste

Directions:

1. Set the Foodi on Sauté mode, add the oil and heat it up. Add the eggplants, salt, pepper, garlic powder and Italian seasoning, toss and cook for 6 minutes
2. Add the coconut milk, tomato paste and all the cheese, set the Foodi on Air Crisp and cook for 10 minutes at 370 °F. Sprinkle the cilantro and the basil on top, divide everything into bowls and serve for breakfast

Apple Pudding

Prep + Cooking Time: 25 minutes, Servings: 4

Ingredients:

- 2 eggs; whisked.
- 1 cup apple, peeled, cored and chopped
- 1 ¼ cups milk
- 2 tbsp. sugar

- ¼ tsp. vanilla extract
- 2 tsp. cinnamon powder
- Cooking spray

Directions:

1. In a bowl mix all the ingredients except the cooking spray and whisk well. Put the reversible rack in the Foodi machine and add the baking pan inside
2. Grease the pan with the cooking spray and pour the apples mix. Set the Foodi on Baking mode and cook the pudding at 360 °F for 15 minutes. Divide into bowls and serve for breakfast.

Artichokes Omelet

Prep + Cooking Time: 20 minutes, Servings: 4

Ingredients:

- 4 eggs; whisked.
- 4 oz. canned artichokes; drained. and chopped
- 4 garlic cloves; minced.
- 1 tbsp. olive oil
- 1 tsp. soy sauce
- Salt and black pepper to the taste

Directions:

1. In a bowl mix all the ingredients except the oil and whisk them well. Add the reversible rack in the Foodi, add the baking pan, grease it with the oil and pour the artichokes mix inside
2. Cook the omelet on Baking mode at 350 °F for 10 minutes. Slice the omelet and serve it for breakfast

Avocado Mix

Prep + Cooking Time: 20 minutes, Servings: 2

Ingredients:

- 4 bacon slices; chopped.
- 2 avocados, peeled, pitted and cut into segments
- 1 tbsp. sriracha sauce
- 1 tbsp. lime juice
- A pinch of salt and black pepper

Directions:

1. Set the Foodi on Sauté mode, heat it up, add the bacon and cook for 4-5 minutes. Add the avocados and all the other ingredients, toss a bit, cook for another 5 minutes, divide into bowls and serve

Yogurt And Spinach Omelet

Prep + Cooking Time: 15 minutes, Servings: 8

Ingredients:

- ½ lb. baby spinach
- 8 eggs; whisked.
- 1 ½ cup Greek yogurt
- ½ cup mint; chopped.
- 2 tbsp. olive oil
- Salt and black pepper to the taste

Directions:

1. In a bowl mix all the ingredients except the oil and whisk well. Add the reversible rack to the Foodi, add the baking pan and pour the eggs mix into the pan
2. Set the Foodi on Baking mode, cook the omelet at 360 °F for 10 minutes, divide between plates and serve for breakfast

Mushrooms And Squash Bowls

Prep + Cooking Time: 15 minutes, Servings: 4

Ingredients:

- 1 red bell pepper, roughly chopped
- 1 yellow squash; cubed.
- 2 green onions, sliced
- 1 cup white mushrooms, sliced
- ½ cup cheddar cheese
- 2 tbsp. olive oil

Directions:

1. Set the Foodi on Sauté mode, add the oil, heat it, up, add the peppers, mushrooms, green onions and the squash, toss and sauté for 5 minutes. Put the pressure lid on, cook everything on High for 5 more minutes, release the pressure fast for 5 minutes, divide into bowls and serve for breakfast

Ninja Toast

Prep + Cooking Time: 11 minutes, Servings: 6

Ingredients:

- 12 bread slices
- 1 cup butter, soft
- ½ cup maple syrup
- 2 tsp. vanilla extract

Directions:

1. In a bowl mix the butter with the syrup and vanilla, whisk and brush the bread slices with this mix. Place the slices in the Foodi's basket and cook on Baking mode at 400 °F for 6 minutes. Serve for breakfast

Mexican Scramble

Prep + Cooking Time: 15 minutes, Servings: 4

Ingredients:

- ½ lb. chorizo; chopped.
- 4 eggs; whisked.
- ½ cup corn
- 1 tbsp. parsley; chopped.
- 1 tbsp. cheddar cheese; grated.
- 1 tbsp. olive oil
- Salt and black pepper to the taste

Directions:

1. Set the Foodi on Sauté mode, add the oil and heat it up. Add the chorizo and the corn, stir and sauté for 5 minutes

2. Add salt, pepper and the eggs, toss, set the Foodi on Air Crisp and cook for another 5 minutes at 360 °F. Add the parsley and the cheese, toss a bit, divide between plates and serve for breakfast

Bacon Patties

Prep + Cooking Time: 13 minutes, Servings: 4

Ingredients:

- 1 puff pastry sheet, rolled and cut into squares
- 8 bacon slices; chopped.
- 4 handful cheddar cheese; grated.
- 4 tsp. mustard

Directions:

1. Divide the cheese, bacon and mustard on half of the pastry sheet squares, top with the other halves, seal the edges and place all the patties in your Foodi's basket
2. Cook everything on Air Crisp for 10 minutes. Divide the patties between plates and serve for breakfast

Potato Frittata

Prep + Cooking Time: 26 minutes, Servings: 6

Ingredients:

- 1 lb. baby potatoes; chopped.
- 1 oz. cheddar cheese; grated.
- ½ cup heavy cream
- 2 red onions; chopped.
- 8 eggs; whisked.
- 1 tbsp. olive oil
- Salt and black pepper to the taste

Directions:

1. In a bowl mix all the ingredients except the oil and toss. Drizzle the oil into the Foodi's baking pan and pour the frittata mixsure inside
2. Put the reversible rack in the machine, add the baking pan and cook on Baking mode at 350 °F for 20 minutes. Divide the frittata between plates and serve for breakfast

Salmon Toast

Prep + Cooking Time: 15 minutes, Servings: 4

Ingredients:

- 16 oz. smoked salmon, skinless, boneless and cut into strips
- 6 cheddar cheese slices
- 2 spring onions; chopped.
- 6 bread slices
- ¼ cup mayonnaise
- 1 tbsp. lime juice
- 3 tbsp. butter, melted
- 2 tbsp. mustard

Directions:

1. In a bowl mix salmon with the mayo, mustard, lime juice and spring onions and stir. Grease the bread slices with the butter and spread the salmon mix on each slice
2. Place the slices in the Foodi's basket and cook on Roast at 400 °F for 5 minutes. Divide the toast between plates and serve for breakfast

Bread Pudding

Prep + Cooking Time: 50 minutes, Servings: 4

Ingredients:

- ¾ cup heavy cream
- 4 eggs; whisked.
- 9 cinnamon buns, cut into quarters
- ½ cup cherries, dried
- 1 tbsp. sugar
- ¼ tsp. cloves, ground
- 2 tsp. orange liqueur

Directions:

1. In a bowl mix all the ingredients and toss. Put the reversible rack in the Foodi, place the baking pan inside and pour the bread pudding inside
2. Set the Foodi on Baking mode and cook the pudding at 325 °F for 40 minutes. Divide into bowls and serve for breakfast

Cauliflower Casserole

Prep + Cooking Time: 30 minutes, Servings: 4

Ingredients:

- 1 cauliflower head, florets separated
- 2 oz. coconut milk
- 2 oz. cheddar cheese; grated.
- 3 eggs
- 2 tsp. parsley; chopped.
- Salt and black pepper to the taste

Directions:

1. Put the cauliflower in the Foodi's baking pan. In a bowl mix all the other ingredients except the parsley, whisk and pour over the cauliflower
2. Add the reversible rack into the Foodi, add the baking pan and cook everything on Baking mode at 350 °F for 20 minutes. Divide between plates and serve for breakfast

Chives Omelet

Prep + Cooking Time: 17 minutes, Servings: 4

Ingredients:

- 4 eggs; whisked.
- 2 tbsp. cheddar cheese; grated.
- 1 tbsp. cilantro; chopped.
- 4 tbsp. coconut cream
-
- 2 tbsp. chives; chopped.
- Cooking spray
- Salt and black pepper to the taste

Directions:

1. In a bowl, mix all the ingredients except the cooking spray and whisk. Add the reversible rack to the Foodi, add the baking pan and grease it with the cooking spray
2. Add the omelet mixsure into the pan and cook on Baking mode at 350 °F for 12 minutes. Divide the omelet between plates and serve

Tofu And Spinach Bowls

Prep + Cooking Time: 15 minutes, Servings: 4

Ingredients:

- 12 oz. firm tofu; cubed.
- 8 oz. baby spinach, torn
- 3 carrots; chopped.
- 1 red bell pepper; chopped.
- 2 cup red quinoa, cooked
- ¼ cup soy sauce
- 2 tbsp. olive oil
- 2 tbsp. lime juice

Directions:

1. Set the Foodi on Sauté mode, add the oil and heat it up. Add the carrots and the bell pepper, stir and sauté for 3 minutes
2. Add the tofu, lime juice, soy sauce, spinach and quinoa, toss, put the pressure lid on and cook on High for 7 minutes. Release the pressure fast for 5 minutes, divide everything into bowls and serve for breakfast.

Broccoli Pudding

Prep + Cooking Time: 25 minutes, Servings: 4

Ingredients:

- 2 cups broccoli florets; chopped.
- ½ cup cheddar cheese, shredded
- ½ cup almonds; chopped.
- ½ cup coconut, shredded
- 3 cups coconut milk

Directions:

1. Put the reversible rack in the Foodi machine and add the baking pan inside. Mix all the ingredients in the baking pan, set the Foodi on Baking mode and cook at 360 °F for 20 minutes. Divide between plates and serve for breakfast

Veggies And Bread Casserole

Prep + Cooking Time: 40 minutes, Servings: 6

Ingredients:

- 1 lb. white bread; cubed.
- ½ lb. cheddar, shredded
- 1 lb. smoked bacon, cooked and chopped
- ½ lb. Monterey jack, shredded
- 1 red onion; chopped.
- 30 oz. canned tomatoes; chopped.
- 8 eggs; whisked.
- ¼ cup avocado oil
- 2 tbsp. chives; chopped.
- 2 tbsp. chicken stock

- Salt and black pepper to the taste

Directions:

1. In the Foodi's baking dish, combine all the ingredients. Add the reversible rack in the machine, add the baking dish and cook the mix on Baking mode at 350 °F for 30 minutes. Divide everything between plates and serve

Sausage Coconut Mix

Prep + Cooking Time: 30 minutes, Servings: 4

Ingredients:

- 4 bacon slices, cooked and crumbled
- 1 lb. breakfast sausage, crumbled
- 2 and ½ cups cheddar cheese, shredded
- 2 eggs
- 2 cups coconut milk
- 3 tbsp. parsley; chopped.
- Cooking spray
- Salt and black pepper to the taste

Directions:

1. In a bowl mix all the ingredients except the cooking spray and toss. Put the reversible rack in the Foodi, place the baking pan inside and grease it with the cooking spray
2. Add the sausage mix in the pan, spread, set the Foodi on Baking mode and cook at 320 °F for 20 minutes. Serve hot for breakfast

Salsa And Cod

Prep + Cooking Time: 21 minutes, Servings: 4

Ingredients:

- 4 cod fillets, skinless, boneless and cubed
- 1 red onion; chopped.
- 1 green bell pepper; chopped.
- ½ cup salsa
-
- 1 cup baby spinach
- 1 cup corn
- A drizzle of olive oil
- 4 tbsp. cheddar; grated.

Directions:

1. Set the Foodi on Sauté mode, add the oil, heat it up, add the onion and sauté for 4 minutes. Add the green bell pepper and the corn, toss and sauté for 4 more minutes
2. Add the fish, salsa and the spinach, put the pressure lid on and cook on High for 8 minutes. Release the pressure fast for 6 minutes, add the cheese, toss, divide everything between plates and serve for breakfast

Chapter3 Vegetable Recipes

Spaghetti Squash and Spinach Walnut Pesto

Prep + Cooking Time: 15 minutes, Servings: 4

Ingredients:

- 1 cup Water
- 4 lb. Spaghetti Squash

For the Pesto

- 1/2 cup spinach, chopped
- 1/3 cup extra virgin olive oil
- 2 Garlic Cloves, minced
- 2 tbsp. Walnuts
- Salt and ground pepper, to taste
- Zest and juice from ½ lemon

Directions:

1. In a food processor put all the pesto ingredients and blend until everything is well incorporated. Season to taste and set aside.
2. Put the squash on a flat surface and use a knife to slice in half lengthwise. Scoop out all seeds and discard them
3. Next, open the Ninja Foodi, pour the water into it and fit the reversible rack at the bottom. Place the squash halves on the rack, close the lid, secure the pressure valve, and select Steam on High pressure for 5 minutes. Press Start/Stop
4. Once the timer has ended, do a quick pressure release, and open the lid
5. Remove the squash halves onto a cutting board and use a fork to separate the pulp strands into spaghetti-like pieces. Return to the pot and close the crisping lid. Cook for 2 minutes on Broil mode
6. Scoop the spaghetti squash into serving plates and drizzle over the spinach pesto

Butter Spaghetti Squash

Prep + Cooking Time: 30 minutes, Servings: 6

Ingredients:

- 1 3- to 3½ lbs. spaghetti squash; halved lengthwise and seeded
- 1/2 cup finely grated Parmesan cheese about 1-ounce
- 2 tbsp. packed fresh sage leaves; minced
- 6 tbsp. unsalted butter
- 1/2 tsp. salt
- 1/2 tsp. ground black pepper

Directions:

1. Put the squash cut side up in the cooker; add 1 cup water.
2. High pressure for 12 minutes. Lock the lid on the Ninja Foodi Multi-cooker and then cook for 12 minutes.

3. To get 12 minutes' cook time, press "Pressure" button and use the Time Adjustment button to adjust the cook time to 12 minutes
4. Pressure Release. Use the quick release method to bring the pot's pressure back to normal
5. Finish the dish. Unlock and open the cooker. Transfer the squash halves to a cutting board; cool for 10 minutes. Discard the liquid in the cooker. Use a fork to scrape the spaghetti-like flesh off the skin and onto the cutting board; discard the skins.
6. Melt the butter in the electric cooker turned to its browning function. Stir in the sage, salt and pepper, then add all of the squash. Stir and toss over the heat until well combined and heated through about 2 minutes. Add the cheese, toss well
7. Close the crisping lid. Select "BROIL" and set the time to 5 minutes. Select START/STOP to begin. Cook until top is browned. Serve.

Braised Red Cabbage and Apples

Prep + Cooking Time: 30 minutes, Servings: 4

Ingredients:

- 1 medium red cabbage about 2 lb.; cored and thinly sliced
- 1 medium tart green apple; such as Granny Smith; peeled, cored and chopped.
- 4 thin bacon slices; chopped.
- 1/2 cup chicken broth
- 1 small red onion; chopped.
- 1 tsp. dried thyme
- 1/4 tsp. ground allspice
- 1/4 tsp. ground mace
- 1 tbsp. balsamic vinegar
- 1 tbsp. packed dark brown sugar

Directions:

1. Fry the bacon in the Ninja Foodi turned to the *air crisp* function, until crisp, about 4 minutes
2. Add the onion to the pot; cook, often stirring, until soft, about 4 minutes. Add the apple, thyme, allspice and mace. Cook about 1 minute, stirring all the while, until fragrant
3. Stir in the brown sugar and vinegar; keep stirring until bubbling, about 1 minute
4. Add the cabbage; toss well to mix evenly with the other ingredients. Drizzle the broth over the cabbage mixture
5. High pressure for 13 minutes. Lock the lid on the Ninja Foodi Multi-cooker and then cook for 13 minutes.
6. To get 13 minutes' cook time, press *Pressure* button and use the Time Adjustment button to adjust the cook time to 13 minutes.
7. Pressure Release. Use the quick release method to return the pot to normal pressure
8. Unlock and open the pot. Close the crisping lid. Select "BROIL" and set the time to 5 minutes. Select START/STOP to begin. Cook until top is browned. Serve.

Zucchini Fries with Marinara Sauce

Prep + Cooking Time: 1 hour and 40 minutes, Servings: 4

Ingredients:

- 2 large zucchinis, cut in sticks 3-inches long and 1/4-inch thick
- 2 tsp. kosher salt
- 2 cups all-purpose flour
- 3 eggs, beaten
- 3 cups seasoned bread crumbs
- 1/4 cup grated Parmesan cheese
- 1 tbsp. garlic powder
- 2 tsp. onion powder
- Marinara sauce, for serving

Directions:

1. Place the zucchini sticks onto a plate and sprinkle with salt. Allow for 15 minutes to remove excess liquid. Pat dry
2. Place flour into a bowl. Place beaten eggs in another bowl. Combine bread crumbs, Parmesan, garlic powder, and onion powder in a third bowl
3. First, dredge fries in the flour, then shake off any excess and coat in the egg. Then coat in bread crumb mixture and return to a clean plate. Repeat with remaining zucchini. Cover plate with plastic wrap and place in the freezer for 30 to 40 minutes.
4. Once coating has hardened, place the Cook & Crisp Basket in the pot. Close crisping lid. Preheat the unit by selecting AIR CRISP, setting the temperature to 360°F, and setting the time to 5 minutes. Press START/STOP to begin.
5. After 5 minutes, open lid and add zucchini fries to basket. Close lid. Select AIR CRISP, set temperature to 360°F, and set time to 24 minutes. Press START/STOP to begin.
6. After 12 minutes, open lid, then lift basket and shake zucchini fries or toss them with silicone-tipped tongs. Lower basket back into pot and close lid to resume cooking
7. After 20 minutes, check fries for desired doneness. Cook for up to 5 more minutes for crispier results. When cooking is complete, serve fries immediately with marinara sauce.

Greens and Beets with Horseradish Sauce

Prep + Cooking Time: 18 minutes, Servings: 4

Ingredients:

- 2 large or 3 small beets with greens; scrubbed and root ends trimmed
- 2 tsp. unsalted butter
- 1 tbsp. minced fresh chives
- 1 cup water; for steaming
- 1 tbsp. whole milk
- 2 tbsp. sour cream
- 1 tsp. prepared horseradish
- 1/4 tsp. lemon zest
- 1/8 tsp. kosher salt; divided.

Directions:

1. Trim off the beet greens and set aside. If the beets are very large 3 inches or more in diameter, quarter them; otherwise, halve them
2. Add the water and insert the steamer basket or trivet. Place the beets on the steamer insert.
3. High pressure for 10 minutes. Lock the lid on the Ninja Foodi Multi-cooker and then cook for 10 minutes.
4. To get 10 minutes' cook time, press *Pressure* button and use the Time Adjustment button to adjust the cook time to 10 minutes.
5. When the timer goes off, turn the cooker off. Warm* setting, turn off
6. Pressure Release. Let the pressure to come down naturally.
7. While the beets are cooking and the pressure is releasing, wash the greens and slice them into 1/2-inch-thick ribbons, removing any tough stems. In a small bowl, whisk together the sour cream, milk, horseradish, lemon zest and ⅟16 tsp. of kosher salt
8. Finish the dish. When the pressure has released completely, unlock and remove the lid. Remove the beets and cool slightly; then use a paring knife or peeler to peel them. Slice them into large bite-size pieces and set aside
9. Remove the steamer from the Ninja Foodi Multi-cooker and pour out the water. Turn the Ninja Foodi Multi-cooker to *Sauté*. Add the butter to melt. When the butter stops foaming, add the beet greens and sprinkle with the remaining ⅟16 tsp. of kosher salt. Cook for 3 to 4 minutes, stirring until wilted.
10. Return the beets to the Ninja Foodi Multi-cooker and heat for 1 or 2 minutes, stirring. Transfer the beets and greens to a platter and drizzle with the sour cream mixture. Sprinkle with the chives and serve
11. It may be tempting to cool the beets entirely before you peel them, but that would be a mistake. Beets are easiest to peel when they're just cool enough to handle; if they get too cold the skins tend to stick.

Smooth Carrots with Pancetta

Prep + Cooking Time: 18 minutes, Servings: 4

Ingredients:

- 1 lb. baby carrots
- 4-ounces pancetta; diced
- 1/4 cup moderately sweet white wine; such as a dry Riesling
- 1 medium leek; white and pale green parts only, sliced lengthwise, washed and thinly sliced
- 1/2 tsp. ground black pepper
- 2 tbsp. unsalted butter; cut into small bits

Directions:

1. Put the pancetta in the Ninja Foodi turned to the *Air crisp* function and use the Time Adjustment button to adjust the cook time to 5 minutes
2. Add the leek; cook, often stirring, until softened. Pour in the wine and scrape up any browned bits at the bottom of the pot as it comes to a simmer
3. Add the carrots and pepper; stir well. Scrape and pour the contents of the Ninja Foodi Multi-cooker into a 1-quart, round, high-sided soufflé or baking dish.
4. Dot with the bits of butter. Lay a piece of parchment paper on top of the dish, then a piece of aluminum foil. Seal the foil tightly over the baking dish.
5. Set the Ninja Foodi Multi-cooker rack inside and pour in 2 cups water. Use aluminum foil to build a sling for the baking dish; lower the baking dish into the cooker.
6. High pressure for 7 minutes. Lock the lid on the Ninja Foodi Multi-cooker and then cook for 7 minutes.
7. To get 7 minutes' cook time, press *Pressure* button and use the Time Adjustment button to adjust the cook time to 7 minutes.
8. Pressure Release. Use the quick release method to return the pot's pressure to normal.
9. Finish the dish. Close the crisping lid. Select "BROIL" and set the time to 5 minutes. Select START/STOP to begin. Cook until top is browned
10. Unlock and open the pot. Use the foil sling to lift the baking dish out of the cooker. Uncover, stir well and serve.

Chickpeas Masala

Prep + Cooking Time: 70 minutes, Servings: 8

Ingredients:

- 1 lb. chickpeas
- 28 oz. canned tomatoes; chopped.
- 14 oz. coconut milk
- 1 yellow onion; chopped.
- A pinch of salt and black pepper
- 6 garlic cloves; minced.
- 1 bunch cilantro; chopped.
- 1 green chili pepper; chopped.
- 2 and ½ cups water
- 4 tbsp. coconut oil, melted
- 1 tbsp. ginger; grated.
- 1 tbsp. cumin, ground

- 1 tsp. chili powder
- 2 tsp. garam masala
- 2 tsp. sugar
- 1 tsp. turmeric powder
- Juice of 2 lemons

Directions:

1. Set the Foodi machine on Sauté mode, add the oil, heat it up, add the onion, salt, pepper and the cumin, stir and sauté for 5 minutes
2. Add the turmeric, garlic, ginger, chili, chili powder and the cilantro, stir and sauté for 2 more minutes. Add the tomatoes, water, coconut milk and the chickpeas, toss, put the pressure lid on and cook on Low for 40 minutes
3. Release the pressure naturally for 10 minutes, add the sugar, garam masala and the lemon juice, toss, set the Foodi on Sauté mode again and cook everything for 5 more minutes. Divide everything into bowls and serve.

Quinoa And Potato Salad

Prep + Cooking Time: 20 minutes, Servings: 4

Ingredients:

- 1 ½ lb. tiny white potatoes; halved
- 1/4 cup white balsamic vinegar
- 1 cup blond white quinoa
- 1 medium shallot; minced
- 2 medium celery stalks; thinly sliced
- 1 large dill pickle; diced
- 1 tbsp. Dijon mustard
- 1 tsp. sweet paprika
- 1/2 tsp. ground black pepper
- 1/4 tsp. celery seeds
- 1/4 tsp. salt
- 1/4 cup olive oil

Directions:

1. Whisk the vinegar, mustard, paprika, pepper, celery seeds and salt in a large serving bowl until smooth; whisk in the olive oil in a thin, steady stream until the dressing is fairly creamy.
2. Place the potatoes and quinoa in the Ninja Foodi Multi-cooker; add enough cold tap water so that the ingredients are submerged by 3 inches some of the quinoa may float
3. High pressure for 10 minutes. Lock the lid on the Ninja Foodi Multi-cooker and then cook for 10 minutes.
4. To get 10 minutes' cook time, press *Pressure* button and use the Time Adjustment button to adjust the cook time to 10 minutes.
5. Pressure Release. Use the quick release method to bring the pot's pressure back to normal.
6. Finish the dish. Unlock and open the pot. Close the crisping lid. Select "BROIL" and set the time to 5 minutes. Select START/STOP to begin
7. Cook until top is browned. Drain the contents of the pot into a colander lined with paper towels or into a fine-mesh sieve in the sink. Do not rinse.
8. Transfer the potatoes and quinoa to the large bowl with the dressing. Add the shallot, celery and pickle; toss gently and set aside for a minute or two to warm up the vegetables

One Pot Pasta Puttanesca

Prep + Cooking Time: 14 minutes, Servings: 4

Ingredients:

- 8-ounces dried whole wheat ziti
- 1 small red onion; chopped.
- 1 tbsp. capers; drained and rinsed, minced
- 1 tbsp. minced garlic
- 1 lb. eggplant, stemmed and diced no need to peel
- 1 28-ounce can diced tomatoes about 3 ½ cups
- 2 medium yellow bell peppers; stemmed, cored and chopped.
- 2 tbsp. olive oil
- 1 ¼ cups vegetable broth
- 2 tbsp. canned tomato paste
- 2 tsp. dried rosemary
- 1 tsp. dried thyme
- 1/2 tsp. ground black pepper

Directions:

1. Heat the oil in the Ninja Foodi Multi-cooker turned to the *Sauté* function. Add the onion, capers and garlic; cook, often stirring, just until the onion first begins to soften, about 2 minutes.
2. Add the eggplant and yellow bell peppers; cook, often stirring, for 1 minute. Mix in the tomatoes, broth, tomato paste, rosemary, thyme and pepper, stirring until the tomato paste coats everything. Stir in the ziti until coated.
3. High pressure for 8 minutes. Lock the lid on the Ninja Foodi Multi-cooker and then cook for 8 minutes.
4. To get 8 minutes' cook time, press *Pressure* button and use the Time Adjustment button to adjust the cook time to 8 minutes
5. Pressure Release. Use the quick release method to drop the pressure in the pot back to normal. Unlock and open the cooker. Stir well before serving

Chickpea Stew with Carrots

Prep + Cooking Time: 28 minutes, Servings: 4

Ingredients:

- 1 9-ounce box frozen artichoke heart quarters; thawed and squeezed of excess moisture
- 1 14-ounce can diced tomatoes about 1 ¾ cups
- 1 lb. baby-carrots; cut into 1-inch pieces
- 6 pitted dates; preferably Medjool, chopped.
- 1 medium red onion; halved and sliced into thin half-moons
- 1 ½ cups dried chickpeas
- 2 cups chicken broth
- 2 tbsp. all-purpose flour
- 2 ½ tbsp. olive oil
- 2 tsp. minced garlic
- 1/2 tsp. ground cinnamon

- 1/2 tsp. ground coriander
- 1/2 tsp. ground cumin
- 1/2 tsp. salt
- 1 tbsp. sweet paprika

Directions:

1. Soak the chickpeas in a big bowl of water for at least 12 hours or up to 16 hours
2. Drain the chickpeas in a colander set in the sink. Whisk the broth and flour in a medium bowl until the flour dissolves.
3. Heat 1 ½ tbsp. oil in the Ninja Foodi Multi-cooker turned to the Sauté function. Add the onion and cook, often stirring, until softened, about 4 minutes
4. Stir in the garlic, paprika, cinnamon, coriander, cumin and salt until aromatic, about 30 seconds. Pour in the tomatoes as well as the broth mixture. Stir well, then add the carrots, dates and drained chickpeas.
5. High pressure for 12 minutes. Lock the lid on the Ninja Foodi Multi-cooker and then cook for 12 minutes.
6. To get 12 minutes' cook time, press *Pressure* button and use the Time Adjustment button to adjust the cook time to 12 minutes
7. Pressure Release. Use the quick release method to drop the pot's pressure back to normal.
8. Finish the dish. Unlock and open the cooker. Heat the remaining tbsp. oil in a large nonstick skillet set over medium-high heat.
9. Add the artichoke heart quarters; fry until brown and crisp, stirring and occasionally turning about 10 minutes. Dish up the chickpea mixture into big bowls and top with the crisp artichoke bits

Vegetable Stew Recipe

Prep + Cooking Time: 55 minutes, Servings: 6

Ingredients:

- 6 cups vegetable stock or beef/chicken stock
- 1/2 cup red wine or rice wine red wine is preferred
- 2 large carrots; cut into bite size pieces
- 3 potatoes cut into chunks
- 4 celery stalks cut into bite size pieces
- 2 cups of sliced white mushrooms
- 1 large onion; diced
- 6 tomatoes; diced
- 3 gloves garlic; minced
- 1 cup pearl barley
- 1 tbsp. dried parsley flakes
- 1 tbsp. dried thyme
- 1 bay leaf

Directions:

1. In a nonstick pan add a drizzle of olive oil and quickly sauté the white mushrooms with the minced garlic and onions until golden brown 2 - 3 minutes on medium heat then add in the red wine and cook for another minute. Set aside.
2. In the Ninja Foodi Multi-cooker add the rest of the ingredients not including the barley.
3. High pressure for 20 minutes. Lock the lid on the Ninja Foodi Multi-cooker and then cook for 20 minutes.

4. To get 20 minutes' cook time, press *Pressure* button and adjust the time
5. Pressure Release. Use the quick release method to bring the pot's pressure back to normal
6. Add the mushrooms and barley, give it a good stir and add 2 pinches of salt and pepper
7. High pressure for 10 minutes. Lock the lid on the Ninja Foodi Multi-cooker and then cook for 10 minutes.
8. To get 10 minutes' cook time, press *Pressure* button and use the Time Adjustment button to adjust the cook time to 10 minutes.
9. Pressure Release. Use the quick release method to bring the pot's pressure back to normal.
10. Finish the dish. At this point the potatoes and carrots should have softened. Add salt and pepper to taste.
11. Serve with your favorite pasta dish fresh baked biscuits

Buffalo Cauliflower Bites

Prep + Cooking Time: 1 hour 20 minutes, Servings: 6

Ingredients:

- 2 heads cauliflower, trimmed, cut in 2-inch florets
- 1 ½ cups water, divided.
- 1 tsp. garlic powder
- 1 tsp. onion powder
- 1 tsp. kosher salt
- 1 ½ cups cornstarch
- 1 tsp. black pepper
- 2 eggs
- 1/2 cup all-purpose flour
- 2 tsp. baking powder
- 1/3 cup buffalo wing sauce

Directions:

1. Place cauliflower and 1/2 cup water into the pot. Assemble pressure lid, making sure the PRESSURE RELEASE valve is in the SEAL position. Select PRESSURE and set to LOW. Set time to 2 minutes. Select START/STOP to begin.
2. When pressure cooking is complete, quick release the pressure by turning the PRESSURE RELEASE valve to the VENT position. Carefully remove lid when unit has finished releasing pressure. Drain cauliflower and chill in refrigerator until cooled, about 10 minutes
3. Whisk together cornstarch, flour, baking powder, garlic powder, onion powder, salt, and pepper. Whisk in eggs and 1 cup water until batter is smooth.
4. Add chilled cauliflower to bowl with batter and gently toss until well coated. Transfer coated cauliflower to baking sheet and chill in freezer for 20 minutes
5. Close crisping lid. Preheat the unit by selecting AIR CRISP, setting the temperature to 360°F, and setting the time to 5 minutes
6. Meanwhile, arrange half the cauliflower in an even layer in the bottom of the Cook & Crisp Basket. After 5 minutes, place basket into the pot.
7. Close crisping lid. Select AIR CRISP, set temperature to 360°F, and set time to 20 minutes. Select START/STOP to begin. When first batch of cauliflower is crisp and golden, transfer to a bowl. Repeat with remaining chilled cauliflower

8. When cooking is complete, microwave hot sauce for 30 seconds, then toss with cooked cauliflower. Serve immediately

Rye Berry and Celery Root Salad

Prep + Cooking Time: 45 minutes, Servings: 4

Ingredients:

- 1 medium celeriac celery root; peeled and shredded through the large holes of a box grater
- 3/4 cup rye berries
- 2 tbsp. honey
- 2 tbsp. apple cider vinegar
- 2 tbsp. unsalted butter
- 1/2 tsp. salt
- 1/2 tsp. ground black pepper

Directions:

1. Place the rye berries in the Ninja Foodi Multi-cooker; pour in enough cold tap water, so the grains are submerged by 2 inches.
2. High pressure for 40 minutes. Lock the lid on the Ninja Foodi Multi-cooker and then cook for 40 minutes.
3. To get 40 minutes' cook time, press *Pressure* button and use the Time Adjustment button to adjust the cook time to 40 minutes.
4. Pressure Release. Use the quick release method to bring the pot's pressure back to normal
5. Finish the dish. Unlock and open the cooker. Stir in the shredded celeriac. Cover the pot without locking it and set aside for 1 minute. Drain the pot into a large colander set in the sink. Wipe out the cooker
6. Melt the butter in the Ninja Foodi Multi-cooker; turned to it sauté function. Add the honey and cook for 1 minute, constantly stirring
7. Add the drained rye berries and celeriac; cook, constantly stirring, for 1 minute. Stir in the vinegar, salt and pepper to serve.

Simple Potato Wedges

Prep + Cooking Time: 45 minutes, Servings: 4

Ingredients:

- 4 Idaho potatoes, cut in 2-inch wedges
- 1 tbsp. fresh oregano leaves, minced
- 4 cloves garlic, peeled, minced
- Juice of 1 lemon
- 2 tbsp. extra virgin olive oil, divided.
- 2 tsp. kosher salt
- 1/2 cup water
- 1 tsp. ground black pepper

Directions:

1. Pour water into the pot. Place potatoes into the Cook & Crisp Basket and place basket into pot
2. Assemble pressure lid, making sure the PRESSURE RELEASE valve is in the SEAL position. Select PRESSURE and set to LOW. Set time to 3 minutes. Select START/STOP to begin.
3. While potatoes are cooking, stir together 1 tbsp. olive oil with oregano, garlic, lemon juice, salt, and pepper in a small bowl. Set aside
4. When pressure cooking is complete, quick release the pressure by moving the PRESSURE RELEASE valve to the VENT position. Carefully remove lid when unit has finished releasing pressure
5. Pour remaining olive oil over the potatoes in the basket, shaking to coat evenly
6. Close the crisping lid. Select AIR CRISP, set temperature to 400°F, and set time to 18 minutes.
7. Select START/STOP to begin. Check potatoes after 12 minutes. Continue cooking for up to 18 minutes for desired crispiness. When cooking is complete, remove potatoes from basket. Toss with oregano dressing and serve

Crispy Ratatouille Recipe

Prep + Cooking Time: 14 minutes, Servings: 4

Ingredients:

- 1 14.5-ounce can diced tomatoes; undrained
- 1 small red bell pepper; cut into ½-inch chunks about 1 cup
- 1 small green bell pepper; cut into ½-inch chunks about 1 cup
- 1 rib celery; sliced about 1 cup
- Kosher salt; for salting and seasoning
- 1 small eggplant; peeled and sliced 1/2-inch thick
- 1 medium zucchini; sliced 1/2-inch thick
- 2 tbsp. olive oil
- 1 cup chopped onion
- 3 garlic cloves; minced or pressed
- 1/2 tsp. dried oregano
- 1/4 tsp. freshly ground black pepper
- 2 tbsp. minced fresh basil
- 1/4 cup water
- 1/4 cup pitted green or black olives optional

Directions:

1. Place a rack on a baking sheet. With kosher salt, very liberally salt one side of the eggplant and zucchini slices and place them, salted-side down, on the rack. Salt the other side.
2. Let the slices sit for 15 to 20 minutes or until they start to exude water you'll see it beading up on the surface of the slices and dripping into the sheet pan. Rinse the slices and blot them dry. Cut the zucchini slices into quarters and the eggplant slices into eighths
3. Turn the Ninja Foodi Multi-cooker to *Sauté*, heat the olive oil until it shimmers and flows like water. Add the onion and garlic and sprinkle with a pinch or two of kosher salt. Cook for about 3 minutes, stirring until the onions just begin to brown
4. Add the eggplant, zucchini, green bell pepper, red bell pepper, celery and tomatoes with their juice, water and oregano
5. High pressure for 4 minutes. Lock the lid on the Ninja Foodi Multi-cooker and then cook for 4 minutes.
6. To get 4 minutes' cook time, press *Pressure* button and use the Time Adjustment button to adjust the cook time to 4 minutes
7. Pressure Release. Use the quick release method
8. Finish the dish. Unlock and remove the lid. Close the crisping lid. Select "BROIL" and set the time to 5 minutes. Select START/STOP to begin. Cook until top is browned
9. Stir in the pepper, basil and olives if using. Taste, adjust the seasoning as needed and serve.
10. While this vegetable dish is usually served on its own, it's great tossed with cooked pasta or served over polenta.

Chapter 4 Beef & Lamb Recipes

Delicious Beef Recipe

Prep + Cooking Time: 30 minutes, Servings: 4

Ingredients:

- 1 ½ lbs. flank steak, sliced
- 4 cups broccoli florets
- 4 scallions; chopped.
- ½ cup beef stock
- ½ cup water
- ½ cup soy sauce
-
- 2 tbsp. brown sugar
- 2 tbsp. cornstarch
- 1 tbsp. ginger; grated.
- 3 tbsp. sherry
- A pinch of salt and black pepper

Directions:

1. In a bowl mix the stock with the soy sauce, sherry, sugar, ginger, salt and pepper and whisk well. Add the steaks, toss and leave aside for 10 minutes
2. Put the water in the Foodi, place the basket inside and put the broccoli in the basket. Put the pressure lid on, set the Foodi to Steam mode, cook the broccoli for 5 minutes and transfer it to a bowl
3. Clean the pot, add the broccoli, the beef, cornstarch and scallions, toss, put the pressure lid on and cook on High for 10 minutes.
4. Release the pressure naturally for 10 minutes, divide everything between plates and serve

Beef And Spinach

Prep + Cooking Time: 30 minutes, Servings: 4

Ingredients:

- 1 lb. beef meat, ground
- 5 oz. baby spinach
- 1 yellow onion; chopped.
- 3 leeks, roughly chopped
- 2 tbsp. tomato puree
- 1 tbsp. olive oil
- Salt and black pepper to the taste

Directions:

1. Set the Foodi on Sauté mode, add the oil and heat it up. Add the onion, stir and cook for 5 minutes. Add the leeks, stir and cook for 2 minutes more
2. Add the beef, salt, pepper, tomato puree and the spinach, toss, put the pressure lid on and cook on High for 10 minutes. Release the pressure naturally for 10 minutes, divide everything into bowls and serve

Easy Short Ribs and Root Vegetables

Prep + Cooking Time: 1 hour 15 minutes, Servings: 6

Ingredients:

- 6 uncooked bone-in beef short ribs about 3 lb., trimmed of excess fat and silver skin
- 2 tsp. kosher salt, divided.
- 3 carrots, peeled, cut in 1-inch pieces
- 3 parsnips, peeled, cut in 1-inch pieces
- 2 tsp. black pepper, divided.
- 3 cloves garlic, peeled, minced
- 1 onion, peeled, chopped.
- 1/4 cup Marsala wine
- 1/4 cup beef broth
- 2 tbsp. brown sugar
- 2 tbsp. fresh thyme, minced, divided.
- 2 tbsp. olive oil, divided.
- 1 cup pearl onions
- 1/4 cup fresh parsley, minced

Directions:

1. Season short ribs on all sides with 1 tsp. salt and 1 tsp. pepper. Select SEAR/SAUTÉ and set to HIGH. Select START/STOP to begin. Heat 1 tbsp. oil in the pot for 3 minutes.
2. After 3 minutes, add short ribs to pot and cook until browned on all sides, about 10 minutes
3. Add onion, wine, broth, brown sugar, garlic, 1 tbsp. thyme, 1/2 tsp. salt, and 1/2 tsp. pepper to pot. Assemble pressure lid, making sure the PRESSURE RELEASE valve is in the SEAL position. Select PRESSURE and set to HIGH. Set time to 40 minutes. Select START/STOP to begin
4. Toss carrots, parsnips, and pearl onions with remaining oil, thyme, salt, and pepper
5. When pressure cooking is complete, quick release the pressure by moving the PRESSURE RELEASE valve to the VENT position. Carefully remove lid when unit has finished releasing pressure.
6. Place the reversible rack inside pot over ribs, making sure rack is in the higher position. Place vegetable mixture on rack. Close crisping lid. Select BAKE/ROAST, set temperature to 350°F, and set time to 15 minutes. Select START/STOP to begin
7. Once vegetables are tender and roasted, transfer them and the ribs to a serving tray and tent loosely with aluminum foil to keep warm
8. Select SEAR/SAUTÉ and set to HIGH. Bring liquid in pot to simmer for 5 minutes. Transfer to bowl and let sit for 2 minutes, then spoon off top layer of fat. Stir in parsley. When cooking is complete, serve sauce with vegetables and ribs.

BBQ Pulled Beef Sandwiches

Prep + Cooking Time: 1 hour, Servings: 2 to 4

Ingredients:

- 2 lb. Beef of choice
- 4 cups finely shredded Cabbage the secret ingredient and you'll never know it's in there.
- 2 cups Water
- 1/2 cup of your favorite BBQ Sauce
- 1 cup Ketchup
- 1/3 cup Worcestershire Sauce
- 1 tbsp. mustard
- 1 tbsp. Horse Radish

Directions:

1. Add and stir in ingredients to your Ninja Foodi Multi-cooker.
2. High pressure for 35 minutes. Lock the lid on the Ninja Foodi Multi-cooker and then cook for 35 minutes.
3. To get 35 minutes' cook time, press *Pressure* button and adjust the time.
4. Pressure Release. Use natural release method. Finish the dish. Remove the lid from the Ninja Foodi Multi-cooker. Close crisping lid. Select *Air Crisp*, set temperature to 390°F and set time to 15 minutes
5. Check after 10 minutes, cooking for an additional 5 minutes if dish needs more browning
6. Set the beef aside. Set the Ninja Foodi Multi-cooker to a *Sauté* mode, Sauté the sauce until it reaches the desired consistency. Serve and Enjoy.

Chinese Style Beef

Prep + Cooking Time: 25 minutes, Servings: 2

Ingredients:

- 1 lb. beef meat, cut into strips
- 1 yellow onion; chopped.
- 8 oz. shiitake mushrooms, sliced
- 2 tbsp. dark soy sauce
- 1 tsp. olive oil
- Salt and black pepper to the taste

Directions:

1. Set the Foodi on Sauté mode, add the oil and heat it up. Add the onion, stir and sauté for 3-4 minutes. Add the mushrooms, soy sauce and the beef, stir and cook for 2-3 minutes more
2. Add salt and pepper, put the pressure lid on and cook on High for 8 minutes. Release the pressure naturally for 10 minutes, divide everything into bowls and serve

Beef Roast

Prep + Cooking Time: 40 minutes, Servings: 4

Ingredients:

- 1 lb. beef roast meat; cubed.
- 1 ½ cups chicken stock
- 2 garlic cloves; minced.
- 1 yellow onion; chopped.
- 3 tbsp. olive oil
- 1 tsp. thyme; chopped.

- Salt and black pepper to the taste

Directions:

1. In your Foodi's baking pan, combine all the ingredients and toss them. Put the reversible rack in the machine, add the baking pan, set the pot on Roast mode and cook at 390 °F for 30 minutes. Divide between plates and serve right away

Pot Roast

Prep + Cooking Time: 1 hour 50 minutes, Servings: 4 to 6

Ingredients:

- 1 3- to 3½ lb. boneless beef chuck roast
- 1 ½ lb. small white or yellow potatoes
- 1/2-ounce dried mushrooms, preferably porcini
- 1 tbsp. olive oil
- 1 large yellow onion, chopped.
- 2 tsp. minced garlic
- 1 ½ cups beef broth
- 3 tbsp. tomato paste
- 1 4-inch rosemary sprig
- 1 tsp. salt
- 1/2 tsp. ground black pepper

Directions:

1. Heat the oil in the Ninja Foodi Multi-cooker. Turn on the Multi-cooker to the Sauté setting then wait for it to boil.
2. Season the roast with the salt and pepper; brown it on both sides, turning once, about 10 minutes. Transfer the meat to a large bowl.
3. Add the onion; cook, often stirring, until translucent, about 4 minutes. Add the garlic; cook, stirring constantly, until aromatic, about 30 seconds. Pour 1 ¼ cup broth in the Ninja Foodi Multi-cooker.
4. Add the tomato paste and stir well until dissolved. Tuck the rosemary into the sauce and crumble in the mushrooms. Nestle the meat into the sauce, adding any juices in the bowl
5. High pressure for 60 minutes. Close the lid and the pressure valve and then cook for 60 minutes
6. To get 60 minutes' cook time, press *Pressure* button and use the Time Adjustment button to adjust the cook time to 60 minutes
7. Pressure Release. Use the quick release method.
8. Unlock and open the cooker; sprinkle the potatoes around the meat
9. High pressure for 30 minutes. Close the lid and the pressure valve again and cook for 30 minutes.
10. To get 30 minutes' cook time, press *Pressure* button
11. Pressure Release. Use the natural release method 20 to 30 minutes
12. Finish the dish. Close crisping lid. Select "BROIL" and set time to 8 minutes. Check after 5 minutes, cooking for an additional 3 minutes if dish needs more browning
13. Transfer the roast to a cutting board; set aside for 5 minutes. Discard the rosemary sprig.
14. Slice the meat into 2-inch irregular chunks and serve these in bowls with the vegetables, mushrooms and broth. Serve

Sausage and Chard Pasta Sauce

Prep + Cooking Time: 18 minutes, Servings: 5 to 6

Ingredients:

- 1-lb. mild Italian pork sausage meat, any casings removed
- 3 small hot chiles, such as cherry peppers or Anaheim chiles, stemmed, seeded and chopped.
- 1 medium red onion, chopped.
- 1/2 cup dry red wine, such as Syrah
- 1/2 cup canned tomato paste
- 1/4 cup chicken broth
- 4 cups stemmed and chopped Swiss chard
- 2 tbsp. olive oil
- 1 tbsp. minced garlic
- 1 tbsp. dried basil
- 2 tsp. dried oregano

Directions:

1. Heat the oil in a Ninja Foodi Multi-cooker, turned to the sauté function.
2. Add the onion and cook, often stirring, until softened, about 4 minutes. Add the chiles and garlic; cook until aromatic, stirring all the while, about 1 minute.
3. Crumble in the sausage meat, breaking up any clumps with a wooden spoon.
4. Stir until it loses its raw color. Stir in the wine, tomato paste, broth, basil and oregano until the tomato paste dissolves. Add the chard and stir well
5. High pressure for 6 minutes. Lock the lid onto the cooker, set the machine's timer to cook at high pressure for 6 minutes
6. To get 6 minutes' cook time, press the *Pressure* button and use the Time Adjustment button to adjust the cook time to 6 minutes.
7. Pressure Release. Use the quick release method to drop the pressure back to normal.
8. Finish the dish. Remove the lid from the Ninja Foodi Multi-cooker. Close crisping lid. Select "BROIL" and set time to 5 minutes
9. Check after 4 minutes, cooking for an additional 4 minutes if dish needs more browning. Stir well before serving

Herbed Beef

Prep + Cooking Time: 25 minutes, Servings: 2

Ingredients:

- 1 lb. beef fillets, cut into strips
- 1 yellow onion; chopped.
- 1 green bell pepper, cut into strips
- ½ tbsp. mustard
- 1 tbsp. olive oil
- 2 tsp. Provencal herbs
- Salt and black pepper to the taste

Directions:

1. Set the Foodi on Sauté mode, add the oil and heat it up. Add the onion and the bell pepper, stir and cook for 5 minutes

2. Add the herbes, salt, pepper, the beef and the mustard, toss, put the pressure lid on and cook on High for 10 minutes. Release the pressure naturally for 10 minutes, divide everything into bowls and serve

Macaroni and Cheese

Prep + Cooking Time: 20 minutes, Servings: 4

Ingredients:

- 1 lb. elbow macaroni
- 1 cup breadcrumbs
- ½ cup bacon; chopped.
- 3 cups chicken stock
- 1 cup water
- 3 cups mozzarella, shredded
- ½ stick of butter, melted
- Salt and black pepper to the taste

Directions:

1. Put the stock, water and the pasta in the Foodi machine, put the pressure lid on and cook on Low for 10 minutes. Release the pressure naturally for 10 minutes.
2. Add the cheese, butter, breadcrumbs, bacon, salt and pepper, toss, leave aside for 10 more minutes, divide between plates and serve

Easy Sausage and Peppers

Prep + Cooking Time: 25 minutes, Servings: 5 to 6

Ingredients:

- 2 ½ lb. sweet Italian sausages in their casings
- 1 medium red onion, halved and thinly sliced
- 2 medium garlic cloves, slivered
- 1 cup red sweet vermouth
- 4 large red bell peppers, stemmed, seeded and cut into strips
- 2 tbsp. olive oil
- 2 tbsp. balsamic vinegar
- 1/4 tsp. grated nutmeg

Directions:

1. Heat the oil in a Ninja Foodi Multi-cooker, turned to the sauté function. Prick the sausages with a fork, add them to the pot and brown on all sides, about 6 minutes. Transfer to a large bowl.
2. Add the peppers and onion; cook, stirring almost constantly, just until the pepper strips glisten, about 2 minutes
3. Add the garlic, cook a few seconds and then stir in the vermouth, vinegar and nutmeg. Nestle the sausages into the mixture.
4. High pressure for 10 minutes. Lock the lid on the Ninja Foodi Multi-cooker and Cook for 10 minutes.
5. To get 10 minutes' cook time, press the *Pressure* button and adjust the time
6. Pressure Release. Use the quick release method to bring the pot's pressure back to normal

7. Remove the lid from the Ninja Foodi Multi-cooker. Close crisping lid. Select *Air Crisp*, set temperature to 390°F and set time to 10 minutes.
8. Check after 8 minutes, cooking for an additional 2 minutes if dish needs more browning. Stir well before serving.

Tex-Mex Meatloaf Recipe

Prep + Cooking Time: 45 minutes, Servings: 8

Ingredients:

- 1 lb. uncooked ground beef
- 1 tbsp. garlic powder
- 2 tsp. ground cumin
- 2 tsp. chili powder
- 1 tsp. cayenne pepper
- 1 egg
- 1 bell pepper, diced
- 2 tsp. kosher salt
-
- 1/4 cup fresh cilantro leaves
- 1/4 barbecue sauce, divided.
- 1/2 jalapeño pepper, seeds removed, minced
- 1 small onion, peeled, diced
- 3 corn tortillas, roughly chopped.
- 1 cup water
- 1 cup corn chips, crushed

Directions:

1. Stir together beef, egg, bell pepper, jalapeño pepper, onion, tortillas, spices, cilantro, and tbsp. barbecue sauce in a large mixing bowl.
2. Place meat mixture in the 8 ½-inch loaf pan and cover tightly with aluminum foil
3. Pour water into pot. Place the loaf pan on the reversible rack, making sure rack is in the lower position. Place rack with pan in pot. Assemble the pressure lid, making sure the PRESSURE RELEASE valve is in the SEAL position
4. Select PRESSURE and set to HIGH. Set time to 15 minutes. Select START/STOP to begin
5. When pressure cooking is complete, quick release the pressure by moving the PRESSURE RELEASE valve to the VENT position. Carefully remove lid when unit has finished releasing pressure
6. Carefully remove foil from loaf pan and close crisping lid. Select BAKE/ROAST, set temperature to 360°F, and set time to 15 minutes. Select START/STOP to begin.
7. While the meatloaf is cooking, stir together the crushed corn chips and 2 tbsp. barbecue sauce in a bowl.
8. After 7 minutes, open lid and top meatloaf with the corn chip mixture. Close lid to resume cooking. When cooking is complete, remove meatloaf from pot and allow to cool for 10 minutes before serving

Lamb and Eggplant Casserole

Prep + Cooking Time: 23 minutes, Servings: 4

Ingredients:

- 1 ½ lb. lean ground lamb
- 1 small eggplant about 3/4 lb., stemmed and diced
- 8-ounces dried spiral-shaped pasta, such as rotini
- 1 tbsp. minced garlic
- 2 tbsp. olive oil
- 1 medium red onion, chopped.
- 1/2 cup canned tomato paste
- 3/4 cup dry red wine, such as Syrah
- 2 ¼ cups chicken broth
- 1/2 tbsp. dried oregano
- 1/2 tsp. dried dill
- 1 tsp. ground cinnamon
- 1/2 tsp. salt
- 1/2 tsp. ground black pepper

Directions:

1. Heat the oil in the Ninja Foodi Multi-cooker turned to the *Sauté* function. Add the onion and cook, often stirring, until softened, about 4 minutes. Add the garlic and cook until aromatic, less than 1 minute.
2. Crumble in the ground lamb; cook, stirring occasionally until it has lost its raw color, about 5 minutes. Add the eggplant and cook for 1 minute, often stirring, to soften a bit. Pour in the red wine and scrape up any browned bits in the pot as it comes to a simmer
3. Stir in the broth, tomato paste, cinnamon, oregano, dill, salt and pepper until everything is coated in the tomato sauce. Stir in the pasta until coated.
4. High pressure for 8 minutes. Lock the lid on the Ninja Foodi Multi-cooker and then cook for 8 minutes.
5. To get 8 minutes' cook time, press *Pressure* button and use the Time Adjustment button to adjust the cook time to 8 minutes
6. Pressure Release. Use the quick release method.
7. Remove the lid from the Ninja Foodi Multi-cooker. Close crisping lid. Select "BROIL" and set time to 5 minutes. Cooking for an additional 4 minutes if dish needs more browning. Unlock and open the pot. Stir well before serving

Beef Bites

Prep + Cooking Time: 20 minutes, Servings: 8

Ingredients:

- 1 lb. beef meat, ground
- 1 egg; whisked.
- 1 yellow onion; chopped.
- 3 tbsp. breadcrumbs
- ½ tsp. garlic; minced.
- Cooking spray
- Salt and black pepper to the taste

Directions:

1. In a bowl mix all the ingredients except the cooking spray, stir well and shape medium meatballs out of this mix

2. Put the meatballs in the Air Crisp basket, grease them with cooking spray, put the basket in the Foodi, set the machine on Air Crisp and cook the meatballs at 390 °F for 15 minutes. Serve the meatballs as an appetizer.

Beef Chili & Cornbread Casserole

Prep + Cooking Time: 60 minutes, Servings: 8

Ingredients:

- 2 lb. uncooked ground beef
- 3 cans 14-ounces each kidney beans, rinsed, drained
- 1 can 28-ounces crushed tomatoes
- 1 cup beef stock
- 1 large white onion, peeled, diced
- 1 green bell pepper, diced
- 1 jalapeño pepper, diced, seeds removed
- 4 cloves garlic, peeled, minced
- 2 tbsp. kosher salt
- 1 tbsp. ground black pepper
- 2 tbsp. ground cumin
- 1 tbsp. onion powder
- 1 tbsp. garlic powder
- 2 cups Cheddar Corn Bread batter, uncooked
- 1 cup shredded Mexican cheese blend
- Sour cream, for serving

Directions:

1. Place beef, beans, tomatoes, and stock into the pot, breaking apart meat. Assemble pressure lid, making sure the PRESSURE RELEASE valve is in the SEAL position. Select PRESSURE and set to HIGH. Set time to 15 minutes. Select START/STOP to begin.
2. When pressure cooking is complete, quick release the pressure by moving the PRESSURE RELEASE valve to the VENT position. Carefully remove lid when unit has finished releasing pressure
3. Select SEAR/SAUTÉ. Set temperature to MD, Select START/STOP. Add onion, green bell pepper, jalapeño pepper, garlic, and spices; stir to incorporate. Bring to a simmer and cook for 5 minutes, stirring occasionally.
4. Dollop corn bread batter evenly over the top of the chili. Close crisping lid. Select BAKE/ROAST, set temperature to 360°F, and set time to 26 minutes. Select START/STOP to begin.
5. After 15 minutes, open lid and insert a wooden toothpick into the center of the corn bread. If corn bread is not done, close lid to resume cooking for another 8 minutes
6. When corn bread is done, sprinkle it with cheese and close lid to resume cooking for 3 minutes, or until cheese is melted. When cooking is complete, top with sour cream and serve

Beef Soup

Prep + Cooking Time: 40 minutes, Servings: 6

Ingredients:

- 2 and ½ lbs. beef stew meat; cubed.
- 15 oz. canned tomatoes; chopped.
- 1 yellow onion; chopped.
- 4 carrots; chopped.

- 4 celery stalks; chopped.
- 6 cups beef stock
- 1 cup pearl barley
- 1 tsp. oregano, dried
- 1 tbsp. olive oil
- 2 tbsp. tomato paste
- A pinch of salt and black pepper

Directions:

1. Set the Foodi on sauté mode, add the oil, heat it up, add the beef, brown it for 5 minutes and transfer to a plate. Add the onion, celery, carrots, oregano, salt and pepper to the machine, stir and cook for another 5 minutes
2. Add the tomatoes, tomato paste, the barley, the stock and the beef, put the pressure lid on and cook on High for 25 minutes. Release the pressure naturally for 10 minutes, divide the soup into bowls and serve

Classic Brisket with Veggies

Prep + Cooking Time: 1 hour 20 minutes, Servings: 4 to 6

Ingredients:

- 2 lb. or larger regular brisket, rinsed and patted dry
- 2 ½ cup homemade beef broth or make from Knorr Beef Base
- 2 tbsp. olive oil
- 5 or 6 red potatoes
- 2 cup large chunks carrots
- 3 tbsp. Worcestershire Sauce
- 4 bay leaves
- Granulated garlic
- Knorr Demi-Glace sauce
- 1/2 cup dehydrated onion
- 2 stalks celery in 1 chunks
- Fresh ground black pepper
- 3 tbsp. heaping chopped garlic
- 1 large yellow onion
- 5 or 6 red potatoes

Directions:

1. Put the Ninja Foodi Multi-cooker on the sauté setting. Put in 1 tbsp. more if needed of the oil and caramelize the onions. Once golden, remove from pot, put in a bowl and set aside. But keep the Ninja Foodi Multi-cooker on the *Sauté* setting.
2. Rub the freshly ground pepper on both sides of the brisket. Do the same with the granulated garlic. Add 1 tbsp. olive oil or more and only lightly sear the brisket on all sides
3. Add back the onions, garlic, Worcestershire sauce, bay leaves, dehydrated onion and beef broth
4. High pressure for 50 minutes. Close the lid and the pressure valve and then cook for 50 minutes
5. To get 50 minutes' cook time, press *Pressure* button and use the Time Adjustment button to adjust the cook time to 50 minutes
6. While the meat is cooking, peel and cut up all the veggies. When the meat is done, use the quick pressure release feature and then remove the lid. Add all of the veggies, replace the lid and cook at high pressure for to 10 minutes.

7. To get 10 minutes' cook time, press *Steam* button
8. Pressure Release. When the time is up, turn the pot off, use the quick release again and remove the lid.
9. Finish the dish. Close crisping lid. Select "“BROIL”" and set time to 8 minutes. Check after 5 minutes, cooking for an additional 3 minutes if dish needs more browning
10. Use a platter to remove the veggies and meat. Use the *Sauté* setting and bring the broth to a boil, then add the Knorr Demi-Glace mixing with a Wisk
11. Adjust seasonings as needed. Serve with Cole Slaw or other salad, homemade rolls or Italian garlic bread. Be sure to remove the bay leaves before serving. Serve and Enjoy

Mouthwatering Beef Stew

Prep + Cooking Time: 1 hour 20 minutes, Servings: 4

Ingredients:

- 1 ½ lb. lean ground beef about 93% lean
- 1 large sweet potato about 1 lb., peeled and shredded through the large holes of a box grater
- 1 tbsp. olive oil
- 1 large yellow onion, chopped.
- 1 tsp. ground cinnamon
- 1 tsp. ground cumin
- 1/2 tsp. dried sage
- 1/2 tsp. dried oregano
- 2 ½ cups beef broth
- 2 tbsp. yellow cornmeal
- 2 tbsp. honey
- 1/2 tsp. salt
- 1/2 tsp. ground black pepper

Directions:

1. Heat the oil in the Ninja Foodi Multi-cooker turned to the Sauté function. Crumble in the ground beef; cook, stirring occasionally, until it loses its raw color and browns a bit, about 5 minutes
2. Add the onion; cook, often stirring, until softened, about 3 minutes
3. Stir in the sweet potato, cinnamon, cumin, sage, oregano, salt and pepper.
4. Cook for 1 minute, stirring constantly. Stir in the cornmeal and honey; cook for 1 minute, often stirring, to dissolve the cornmeal. Stir in the broth
5. High pressure for 5 minutes. Lock the lid on the Ninja Foodi Multi-cooker and then cook for 5 minutes.
6. To get 5 minutes' cook time, press *Pressure* button and use the Time Adjustment button to adjust the cook time to 5 minutes.
7. Pressure Release. Use the quick release method to drop the pot's pressure to normal.
8. Finish the dish. Remove the lid from the Ninja Foodi Multi-cooker. Close crisping lid. Select *Air Crisp*, set temperature to 390°F and set time to 20 minutes
9. Check after 15 minutes, cooking for an additional 15 minutes if dish needs more browning. Stir well and set aside, loosely covered, for 5 minutes before serving

Delightful Lamb Shanks with Pancetta

Prep + Cooking Time: 1 hour 55 minutes, Servings: 4

Ingredients:

- 1 28-ounce can diced tomatoes, drained about 3 ½ cups
- 4 12-ounce lamb shanks
- 1 6-ounce pancetta chunk, chopped.
- 2 cups dry, light white wine, such as Sauvignon Blanc
- 1-ounce dried mushrooms, preferably porcini, crumbled
- 2 tbsp. olive oil
- 1 small yellow onion, chopped.
- 3 tbsp. packed celery leaves, minced
- 2 tbsp. minced chives
- 2 tbsp. all-purpose flour
- 1/2 tsp. ground black pepper

Directions:

1. Heat the oil in the Ninja Foodi Multi-cooker, turned to the *Sauté* function. Add the pancetta and brown well, about 6 minutes, stirring often. Use a slotted spoon to transfer the pancetta to a large bowl
2. Add two of the shanks to the cooker; brown on all sides, turning occasionally, about 8 minutes. Transfer them to the bowl and repeat with the remaining shanks.
3. Add the onion to the pot; cook, often stirring, until softened, about 4 minutes. Stir in the tomatoes, dried mushroom crumbles, celery leaves and chives. Cook until bubbling, about minutes, stirring often
4. Whisk the wine, flour and pepper in a medium bowl until the flour dissolves; stir this mixture into the sauce in the pot. Cook until thickened and bubbling, about 1 minute
5. Return the shanks, pancetta and their juices to the cooker.
6. High pressure for 60 minutes. Close the lid and the pressure valve and then cook for 60 minutes
7. To get 60 minutes' cook time, press *Pressure* button and use the Time Adjustment button to adjust the cook time to 60 minutes
8. Turn off the Ninja Foodi Multi-cooker or unplug it, so it doesn't jump to its keep-warm setting
9. Pressure Release. Let its pressure return to normal naturally, 20 to 30 minutes
10. Finish the dish. Remove the lid from the Ninja Foodi Multi-cooker. Close crisping lid. Select *Air Crisp*, set temperature to 375°F and set time to 18 minutes. Check after 10 minutes, cooking for an additional 8 minutes if dish needs more browning.
11. Transfer a shank to each serving bowl. Skim any surface fat from the sauce with a flatware spoon. Ladle the sauce and vegetables over the lamb shanks

Chapter 5 Pork Recipes

Delicious Braised Pork Neck Bones

Prep + Cooking Time: 40 minutes, Servings: 6

Ingredients:

- 3 lbs. Pork Neck Bones
- 4 tbsp. Olive Oil
- 1 White Onion, sliced
- 1/2 cup Red Wine
- 2 cloves Garlic, smashed
- 1 tbsp. Tomato Paste
- 1 tsp. dried Thyme
- 1 cup Beef Broth
- Salt and Black Pepper to taste

Directions:

1. Open the lid and select Sear/Sauté mode. Warm the olive oil
2. Meanwhile season the pork neck bones with salt and pepper. After, place them in the oil to brown on all sides. Work in batches.
3. Each batch should cook in about 5 minutes. Then, remove them onto a plate.
4. Add the onion and season with salt to taste. Stir with a spoon and cook the onions until soft, for a few minutes. Then, add garlic, thyme, pepper, and tomato paste. Cook them for 2 minutes, constant stirring to prevent the tomato paste from burning
5. Next, pour the red wine into the pot to deglaze the bottom. Add the pork neck bones back to the pot and pour the beef broth over it
6. Close the lid, secure the pressure valve, and select Pressure mode on High pressure for 10 minutes. Press Start/Stop to start cooking.
7. Once the timer has ended, let the pot sit for 10 minutes before doing a quick pressure release. Close the crisping lid and cook on Broil mode for 5 minutes, until nice and tender.
8. Dish the pork neck into a serving bowl and serve with the red wine sauce spooned over and a right amount of broccoli mash

Oregano Meatballs

Prep + Cooking Time: 30 minutes, Servings: 6

Ingredients:

- 1 lb. pork meat; minced.
- 1 cup tomato puree
- ½ tbsp. lime peel; grated.
- 1 tbsp. oregano; chopped.
- 1 tbsp. bread crumbs
- 2 tbsp. parmesan; grated.
- Salt and black pepper to the taste

Directions:

1. In a bowl mix all the ingredients except the tomato puree, stir well and shape medium meatballs out of this mix. Set the Foodi on Sauté mode, add the meatballs and brown them for 3 minutes
2. Add the tomato puree, toss a bit, put the pressure lid on and cook on High for 15 minutes. Release the pressure naturally for 10 minutes, divide the meatballs into bowls and serve as an appetizer

Paprika Pork Chops

Prep + Cooking Time: 25 minutes, Servings: 6

Ingredients:

- 4 medium pork chops
- 2 garlic cloves; minced.
- ¼ cup olive oil
- 1 tbsp. sweet paprika
- Salt and black pepper to the taste

Directions:

1. In a bowl mix the all the ingredients and toss. Put the pork chops in the Foodi's basket, set the machine on Air Crisp and cook at 400 °F for 15 minutes. Divide the chops between plates and serve.

Pork Shoulder Chops With Carrots

Prep + Cooking Time: 70 minutes, Servings: 4 to 6

Ingredients:

- 3 lb. bone in pork shoulder chops, each 1/2 to 3/4 inch thick
- 6 medium carrots
- 1/3 cup maple syrup
- 1/3 cup chicken broth

- 3 medium garlic cloves
- 1 tbsp. bacon fat
- 1/3 cup soy sauce
- 1/2 tsp. ground black pepper

Directions:

1. Melt the bacon fat in a Ninja Foodi Multi-cooker, turned to the browning function. Add about half the chops and brown well, turning once, about 5 minutes. Transfer these to a large bowl and brown the remaining chops
2. Stir the carrots and garlic into the pot; cook for 1 minute, constantly stirring. Pour in the soy sauce, maple syrup and broth, stirring to dissolve the maple syrup and to get up any browned bits on the bottom of the pot. Stir in the pepper. Return the shoulder chops and their juices to the pot. Stir to coat them in the sauce
3. High pressure for 40 minutes. Lock the lid on the Ninja Foodi Multi-cooker and then cook for 40 minutes
4. To get 40 minutes' cook time, press *Pressure* button and use the Time Adjustment button to adjust the cook time to 40 minutes.
5. Pressure Release. Let the pressure to come down naturally for at least 14 to 16 minutes, then quick release any pressure left in the pot
6. Finish the dish. Close crisping lid and select Broil, set time to 7 minutes.
7. Transfer the chops, carrots and garlic cloves to a large serving bowl. Skim the fat off the sauce and ladle it over the servings.

Cinnamon Pork

Prep + Cooking Time: 30 minutes, Servings: 4

Ingredients:

- 1 lb. pork stew meat; cubed.
- 1 yellow onion; chopped.
- 1 garlic clove; minced.
- 2 tbsp. olive oil
- 3 tbsp. parsley; chopped.
- 1 tsp. cinnamon powder
- Salt and black pepper to the taste

Directions:

1. Set the Foodi on Sauté mode, add the oil and heat it up. Add the onion, stir and sauté for 5 minutes. Add the meat, garlic, cinnamon, salt and pepper, toss and sauté for 4-5 minutes more
2. Add the parsley, put the pressure lid on and cook on High for 12 minutes more. Release pre pressure naturally for 10 minutes, divide everything into bowls and serve

Chinese Pork

Prep + Cooking Time: 90 minutes, Servings: 8

Ingredients:

- 3 lbs. pork shoulder roast
- 4 garlic cloves; minced.
- ¼ cup ketchup
- ¼ cup soy sauce
- ½ cup chicken stock
- ½ cup hoisin sauce
- ½ cup honey
- 1 tsp. Chinese five spice powder
- 4 tsp. ginger; grated.

Directions:

1. Combine all the ingredients in the Foodi machine, put the pressure lid on and cook on High for 1 hour and 20 minutes. Release the pressure naturally for 10 minutes, divide everything between plates and serve

Honey Mustard Pork Tenderloin Recipe

Prep + Cooking Time: 30 minutes, Servings: 4

Ingredients:

- 2 lbs. Pork Tenderloin
- 1 tbsp. Worcestershire Sauce
- 1/2 tbsp. Cornstarch
- 1/2 cup Chicken Broth
- 1/4 cup Balsamic Vinegar
- 1 clove Garlic, minced
- 2 tbsps. Olive Oil
- 1/4 cup Honey
- 1 tsp. Sage Powder
- 1 tbsp. Dijon Mustard
- 4 tbsp. Water
- Salt and Black Pepper to taste
- Brussels sprouts, sautéed

Directions:

1. Put the pork on a clean flat surface and pat dry using paper towels. Season with salt and pepper. Select Sear/Sauté mode.
2. Heat the oil and brown the pork on both sides, for about 4 minutes in total. Remove the pork onto a plate and set aside

3. Add in honey, chicken broth, balsamic vinegar, garlic, Worcestershire sauce, mustard, and sage powder. Stir the ingredients and return the pork to the pot
4. Close the lid, secure the pressure valve, and select Pressure mode on High for 15 minutes. Once the timer has ended, do a quick pressure release. Remove the pork with tongs onto a plate and wrap it in aluminum foil
5. Next, mix the cornstarch with water and pour it into the pot. Select Sear/Sauté mode, stir the mixture and cook until it thickens. Then, turn the pot off after the desired thickness is achieved.
6. Unwrap the pork and use a knife to slice it with 3 to 4-inch thickness. Arrange the slices on a serving platter and spoon the sauce all over it. Serve with a syrupy sautéed Brussels sprouts.

BBQ Pork with Ginger Coconut and Sweet Potatoes

Prep + Cooking Time: 40 minutes, Servings: 4

Ingredients:

- 4 frozen uncooked boneless pork chops 8-ounces each
- 3 sweet potatoes, peeled, cut in 1-inch cubes
- 1/2 cup unsweetened coconut milk
- 1 tsp. Chinese five spice powder
- 1/2 stick 1/4 cup butter
- 1 tbsp. fresh ginger, peeled, minced
- 1/4 cup hoisin sauce
- 1/3 cup honey
- 1 ½ tbsp. soy sauce
- 1 tsp. kosher salt
- 1/2 tsp. white pepper

Directions:

1. Place sweet potatoes and coconut milk into the pot. Place reversible rack inside pot over sweet potatoes, making sure rack is in the higher position.
2. Place pork chops on rack. Assemble pressure lid, making sure the PRESSURE RELEASE valve is in the SEAL position. Select PRESSURE and set to HIGH. Set time to 4 minutes. Select START/STOP to begin.
3. While pork chops and sweet potatoes are cooking, whisk together hoisin sauce, honey, soy sauce, and Chinese five spice powder.
4. When pressure cooking is complete, quick release the pressure by moving the PRESSURE RELEASE valve to the VENT position. Carefully remove lid when unit has finished releasing pressure
5. Remove rack with pork from pot. Mash sweet potatoes with butter, ginger, and salt, using a mashing utensil that won't scratch the nonstick surface of the pot
6. Place rack with pork back in pot and brush top of pork generously with 1/2 of sauce mixture.

7. Close crisping lid. Select BROIL and set time to 15 minutes. Select START/STOP to begin. After 5 minutes, open lid, flip pork chops, then brush them with remaining sauce.
8. Close lid to resume cooking. Check after 10 minutes and remove if desired doneness is achieved. If not, cook up to 5 more minutes, checking frequently. When cooking is complete, remove pork from rack and allow to rest for 5 minutes before serving with mashed potatoes

Special Biscuits

Prep + Cooking Time: 40 minutes, Servings: 6

Ingredients:

- 12 oz. pork sausage, crumbled
- 16 oz. biscuit dough
- ½ cup cheddar cheese, shredded
- 3 cups milk
- ¼ cup white flour
- 2 tbsp. butter
- A pinch of salt and black pepper

Directions:

1. Set the Foodi on Sauté mode, heat it up, add the sausage, salt and pepper, stir and cook for 5 minutes. Add the butter, milk and the flour, whisk well and cook for 7 minutes.
2. Meanwhile, separate each biscuit and fill each with the cheddar cheese. Put the reversible rack in the Foodi, place the biscuits in on the rack and lower it into the gravy
3. Set the machine on Baking mode and cook the biscuits at 325 °F for 15 minutes. Divide the biscuits between plates, drizzle the gravy all over and serve as a side

Pork Loin and Apples

Prep + Cooking Time: 43 minutes, Servings: 8

Ingredients:

- 1 3 lb. boneless pork loin roast
- 1 large red onion, halved and thinly sliced
- 2 medium tart green apples, such as Granny Smith, peeled, cored and thinly sliced
- 1/2 cup moderately sweet white wine, such as Riesling
- 2 tbsp. unsalted butter
- 1/4 cup chicken broth
- 4 fresh thyme sprigs
- 2 bay leaves
- 1/2 tsp. salt
- 1/2 tsp. ground black pepper

Directions:

1. Melt the butter in the Ninja Foodi Multi-cooker, set on the *Sauté* function. Add the pork loin and brown it on all sides, turning occasionally, about 8 minutes in all. Transfer to a large plate.
2. Add the onion to the pot; cook, often stirring, until softened, about 3 minutes. Stir in the apple, thyme and bay leaves. Pour in the wine and scrape up any browned bits on the bottom of the pot
3. Pour in the broth; stir in the salt and pepper. Nestle the pork loin into this apple mixture; pour any juices from the plate into the pot.
4. High pressure for 30 minutes. Lock the lid on the Ninja Foodi Multi-cooker and then cook for 30 minutes.
5. To get 30 minutes' cook time, press *Pressure* button and adjust the time
6. Pressure Release. Use the quick release method to bring the pot's pressure to normal
7. Finish the dish. Close crisping lid and select Broil, set time to 7 minutes.
8. Transfer the pork to a cutting board; let stand for 5 minutes while you dish the sauce into serving bowls or onto a serving platter. Slice the loin into 1/2-inch-thick rounds and lay these over the sauce.

Pork Meatballs

Prep + Cooking Time: 25 minutes, Servings: 12

Ingredients:

- 1 lb. pork meat, ground
- 2 garlic cloves; minced.
- ½ cup bread crumbs
- 2 cups sweet and sour sauce
- ½ cup pineapple; chopped.
- 1 cup scallions; chopped.
- 1 egg; whisked.
- 1 tbsp. ginger; grated.
- 1 tbsp. mustard
- 2 tbsp. soy sauce
- 1 tsp. coriander, ground
- Juice of 1 lime

Directions:

1. In a bowl combine all the ingredients except the sauce, stir well and shape medium meatballs out of this mix
2. Put the meatballs in your Foodi, add the sweet and sour sauce, toss gently, put the pressure lid on and cook the meatballs on High for 15 minutes. Release the pressure naturally for 10 minutes, divide the meatballs into bowls and serve

Simple Spare Ribs with Wine

Prep + Cooking Time: 75 minutes, Servings: 4

Ingredients:

- 1 lb. pork spare ribs, cut into pieces
- 1 tbsp. corn starch
- 1 tbsp. olive oil
- 1 – 2 tsp. water
- Green onions as garnish
- 1 tsp. fish sauce optional

Black Bean Marinade:

- 3 cloves garlic, minced
- 1 tsp. sesame oil
- 1 tsp. sugar
- 1 tbsp. ginger, grated
- 1 tbsp. black bean sauce
- 1 tbsp. light soy sauce
- A pinch of white pepper

Directions:

1. Marinate the pork spare ribs with Black Bean Marinade in an oven-safe bowl. Then, sit it in the fridge for 25 minutes.
2. First, mix 1 tbsp. of olive oil into the marinated spare ribs. Then, add 1 tbsp. of cornstarch and mix well. Finally, add 1 – 2 tsp. of water into the spare ribs and mix well
3. Add 1 cup of water into the Ninja Foodi Multi-cooker. Place steam rack in the Ninja Foodi Multi-cooker. Then, put the bowl of spare ribs on the rack
4. High pressure for 15 minutes. Lock the lid on the Ninja Foodi Multi-cooker and then cook for 15 minutes.
5. To get 15 minutes' cook time, press *Pressure* Button and then adjust the time
6. Pressure Release. Let the pressure to come down naturally for at least 15 minutes, then quick release any pressure left in the pot.
7. Finish the dish. Close crisping lid. Select *Air Crisp*, set temperature to 375°F and set time to 10 minutes. Check after 5 minutes, cooking for an additional 5 minutes if dish needs more browning
8. Taste and add one tsp. of fish sauce and green onions as garnish if you like. Serve immediately.

Yummy Pork Chops

Prep + Cooking Time: 35 minutes, Servings: 6

Ingredients:

- 1 lb. pork chops

- 3 cups chicken stock
- 1 garlic clove; minced.
- 1 ½ cups heavy cream
- 2 yellow onions; chopped.
- 1 tbsp. olive oil
- 2 tbsp. sweet paprika
- 2 tbsp. dill; chopped.
- Salt and black pepper to the taste

Directions:

1. Put the pork chops in your Foodi's basket, season with salt, pepper, garlic and the paprika, rub, set the machine on Air Crisp and cook at 380 °F for 10 minutes. Transfer the pork chops to the Foodi's baking pan, add all the other ingredients and toss
2. Place the baking pan in the machine, set it on Baking mode and cook at 370 °F for 15 minutes more. Divide everything between plates and serve hot

Delicious Pulled Pork Sandwiches

Prep + Cooking Time: 60 minutes, Servings: 8

Ingredients:

- 2 ½ – 3 lb. uncooked boneless pork shoulder, cut in 1-inch cubes
- 1 can 6-ounces tomato paste
- 2 tbsp. barbecue seasoning
- 1 cup apple cider vinegar
- 1 tbsp. garlic powder
- 2 tsp. kosher salt
- Coleslaw and Potato rolls for servings

Directions:

1. Add pork, spices, and vinegar to the pot. Assemble pressure lid, making sure the pressure release valve is in the SEAL position. Select PRESSURE and set to HIGH. Set time to 35 minutes. Select START/STOP to begin
2. When pressure cooking is complete, quick release the pressure by turning the pressure release valve to VENT position. Carefully remove lid when unit has finished releasing pressure.
3. Select SEAR/SAUTÉ and set to MEDIUM-HIGH. Select START/STOP to begin
4. Add tomato paste and stir to incorporate. Allow pork to simmer for 10 minutes, or until the liquid has reduced by half, as shown above, stirring occasionally with a wooden spoon or silicone tongs to shred the pork.
5. Serve pulled pork on potato rolls topped with coleslaw.

Garlic Pork Chops

Prep + Cooking Time: 30 minutes, Servings: 4

Ingredients:

- 4 pork chops
- 4 garlic cloves; minced.
- 2 tbsp. rosemary; chopped.
- 2 tbsp. olive oil
- Salt and black pepper to the taste

Directions:

1. In a bowl mix all the ingredients and toss them well. Put the reversible rack in the Foodi and add the basket inside
2. Add the pork chops to the basket, set the machine on Air Crisp and cook at 400 °F for 20 minutes. Serve with a side salad.

Buttery Pork Steaks

Prep + Cooking Time: 24 minutes, Servings: 4

Ingredients:

- 4 pork steaks
- 2 tbsp. butter, melted
- 1 tbsp. smoked paprika
- Salt and black pepper to the taste

Directions:

1. In a bowl mix all the ingredients and toss them. Put the steaks in the Foodi's basket, set the machine on Air Crisp and cook at 390 °F for 7 minutes on each side. Divide the steaks between plates and serve

Garlic Pork

Prep + Cooking Time: 35 minutes, Servings: 4

Ingredients:

- 1 ½ lbs. pork stew meat; cubed.
- 1 tbsp. smoked paprika
- 3 tbsp. olive oil
- 3 tbsp. garlic; minced.
- Salt and black pepper to the taste

Directions:

1. In the Foodi's baking pan, combine all the ingredients and toss. Put the reversible rack in the machine, add the baking pan inside, set the pot on Roast mode and cook at 390 °F for 25 minutes. Divide everything between plates and serve with a side salad

Pork Chops

Prep + Cooking Time: 25 minutes, Servings: 4

Ingredients:

- 2 lbs. pork chops, boneless
- 1 green cabbage head, shredded
- 2 cups chicken stock
- A pinch of salt and black pepper
- 2 tbsp. butter, melted

Directions:

1. Put all the ingredients in the Foodi machine, put the pressure lid on and cook on High for 15 minutes. Release the pressure naturally for 10 minutes, divide everything between plates and serve

Rosemary Sausage and Onion

Prep + Cooking Time: 35 minutes, Servings: 4

Ingredients:

- 6 pork sausage links, halved
- 2 yellow onion, sliced
- 2 garlic cloves; minced.
- 1 tbsp. rosemary; chopped.
- 1 tbsp. olive oil
- 1 tbsp. sweet paprika
- Salt and black pepper to the taste

Directions:

1. In your Foodi's baking pan, combine all the ingredients and toss. Put the reversible rack in the Foodi, add the baking pan, set the machine on Baking mode and cook at 370 °F for 25 minutes. Divide between plates and serve

Pork Carnitas

Prep + Cooking Time: 55 minutes, Servings: 4

Ingredients:

- 2 lbs. pork butt; cubed.
- 1 yellow onion; chopped.
- 6 garlic cloves; minced.
- ½ cup chicken stock
- Juice of 1 orange
- A pinch of salt and black pepper

- ½ tsp. oregano, dried
- ½ tsp. cumin, ground

Directions:

1. Put all the ingredients in the Ninja Foodi machine, put the pressure lid on and cook on High for 20 minutes.
2. Release the pressure fast for 4 minutes, set the machine on Sauté mode and cook everything for 15 minutes more. Set the Foodi on Broil mode, cook everything for 8 more minutes. Divide everything into bowls and serve

Ninja Pulled Pork

Prep + Cooking Time: 2 hour 5 minutes, Servings: 10

Ingredients:

- 1 4- to 4½ lb. bone in skinless pork shoulder, preferably pork butt
- Up to 1 ½ cups light-colored beer, preferably a pale ale or amber lager
- 1/2 tsp. garlic powder
- 1/2 tsp. ground cloves
- 1/2 tsp. ground cinnamon
- 2 tbsp. smoked paprika
- 2 tbsp. packed dark brown sugar
- 1 tbsp. ground cumin
- 1/2 tbsp. dry mustard
- 1 tsp. ground coriander
- 1 tsp. dried thyme
- 1 tsp. onion powder
- 1 tsp. salt
- 2 tsp. ground black pepper

Directions:

1. Mix the smoked paprika, brown sugar, cumin, pepper, mustard, coriander, thyme, onion powder, salt, garlic powder, cloves and cinnamon in a small bowl. Massage the mixture all over the pork.
2. Set the pork in the Ninja Foodi Multi-cooker. Pour 1cup beer into the electric cooker without knocking the spices off the meat
3. High pressure for 80 minutes. Lock the lid on the Ninja Foodi Multi-cooker and then cook for 80 minutes.
4. To get 80 minutes' cook time, press *Pressure* button and use the Time Adjustment button to adjust the cook time to 80 minutes.
5. Pressure Release. Let its pressure fall to normal naturally, 25 to 35 minutes
6. Finish the dish. Close crisping lid and select Broil, set time to 7 minutes

7. Transfer the meat to a large cutting board. Let stand for 5 minutes. Use a spoon to skim as much fat off the sauce in the pot as possible
8. Set the *Sauté* function. Bring the sauce to a simmer, stirring occasionally; continue boiling the sauce, often stirring, until reduced by half, 7 to 10 minutes.
9. Use two forks to shred the meat off the bones; discard the bones and any attached cartilage. Pull any large chunks of meat apart with the forks and stir the meat back into the simmering sauce to reheat. Serve and Enjoy!

Amazing Pork Chops with Applesauce

Prep + Cooking Time: 50 minutes, Servings: 4

Ingredients:

- 2 to 4 pork loin chops we used center cut, bone-on
- 2 gala apples, thinly sliced
- 1 tsp. cinnamon powder
- 1 tbsp. honey
- 1/2 cup unsalted homemade chicken stock or water
- 1 tbsp. grapeseed oil or olive oil
- 1 small onion, sliced
- 3 cloves garlic, roughly minced
- 2 tbsp. light soy sauce
- 1 tbsp. butter
- Kosher salt and ground black pepper to taste
- 2 pieces whole cloves optional
- 1 ½ tbsp. cornstarch mixed with 2 tbsp. water optional

Directions:

1. Make a few small cut around the sides of the pork chops so they will stay flat and brown evenly
2. Season the pork chops with a generous amount of kosher salt and ground black pepper.
3. Heat up your Ninja Foodi Multi-cooker. Add grapeseed oil into the pot. Add the seasoned pork chops into the pot, then let it brown for roughly 2 – 3 minutes on each side. Remove and set aside.
4. Add the sliced onions and stir. Add a pinch of kosher salt and ground black pepper to season if you like. Cook the onions for roughly 1 minute until softened. Then, add garlic and stir for 30 seconds until fragrance
5. Add in the thinly sliced gala apples, whole cloves optional and cinnamon powder, then give it a quick stir. Add the honey and partially deglaze the bottom of the pot with a wooden spoon
6. Add chicken stock and light soy sauce, then fully deglaze the bottom of the pot with a wooden spoon. Taste the seasoning and add more salt and pepper if desired

7. Place the pork chops back with all the meat juice into the pot
8. High pressure for 10 minutes. Lock the lid on the Ninja Foodi Multi-cooker and then cook for 10 minutes.
9. To get 10 minutes' cook time, press *Pressure* button and use the Time Adjustment button to adjust the cook time to 10 minutes
10. Pressure Release. Let it fully natural release roughly 10 minutes. Open the lid carefully.
11. Finish the dish. Close crisping lid. Select *Air Crisp*, set temperature to 375°F and set time to 10 minutes. Check after 10 minutes, cooking for an additional 5 minutes if dish needs more browning
12. Remove the pork chops and set aside. Turn the Multi-cooker to the Sauté setting. Remove the cloves and taste the seasoning one more time.
13. Add more salt and pepper if desired. Add butter and stir until it has fully dissolved into the sauce
14. Mix the cornstarch with water and mix it into the applesauce one third at a time until desired thickness.
15. Drizzle the applesauce over the pork chops and serve immediately with side dishes!

Peppers and Pork Stew

Prep + Cooking Time: 30 minutes, Servings: 4

Ingredients:

- 1 large yellow or white onion, chopped.
- 1 large green bell pepper, stemmed, cored and cut into 1/4-inch-thick strips
- 1 lb. boneless center-cut pork loin chops, cut into 1/4-inch-thick strips
- 1 large red bell pepper, stemmed, cored and cut into 1/4-inch-thick strips
- 1 14-ounce can diced tomatoes, drained about 1 3/4 cups
- 2 tsp. minced, seeded fresh jalapeño chile
- 2 tsp. dried oregano
- 2 tbsp. olive oil
- 2 tsp. minced garlic
- 2 ½ cups canned hominy drained and rinsed
- 1 cup chicken broth

Directions:

1. Heat the oil in a Ninja Foodi Multi-cooker, turned to the Sauté function. Add the onion and both bell peppers; cook, often stirring, until the onion softens, about 4 minutes.
2. Add the garlic, jalapeño and oregano; stir well until aromatic, less than 20 seconds. Add the hominy, tomatoes, broth and pork; stir over the heat for 1 minute
3. High pressure for 12 minutes. Lock the lid on the Ninja Foodi Multi-cooker and then cook for 12 minutes.

4. To get 12 minutes' cook time, press *Pressure* button and use the Time Adjustment button to adjust the cook time to 12 minutes.
5. Pressure Release. Use the quick release method to bring the pot's pressure back to normal. Unlock and open the cooker. Stir well before serving

Smoked Pork

Prep + Cooking Time: 40 minutes, Servings: 6

Ingredients:

- 2 and ½ lbs. pork loin, boneless and cubed
- ¾ cup beef stock
- 1 tbsp. smoked paprika
- 2 tbsp. olive oil
- ½ tbsp. garlic powder
- 1 tsp. oregano, dried
- 1 tsp. basil, dried
- Salt and black pepper to the taste

Directions:

1. In your Foodi's baking pan, combine all the ingredients and toss. Put the reversible rack in the machine, add the baking pan, set the pot on Roast mode and cook at 370 °F for 30 minutes. Divide everything between plates and serve

Chapter 6 Poultry Recipes

Black Bean Soup

Prep + Cooking Time: 70 minutes, Servings: 6

Ingredients:

- 2 yellow onions; chopped.
- 2 cups black beans
- 5 cups water
- 1 cup brewed coffee
- 1 cup sour cream
- Zest and juice of 1 lime
- 1 red bell pepper; chopped.
- 1 jalapeno pepper; chopped.
- 4 garlic cloves; minced.
- 2 bay leaves
- 2 celery stalks; chopped.
- 1 tbsp. tomato paste
- 3 tbsp. canola oil
- 1 tbsp. cumin, ground
- A pinch of salt and black pepper

Directions:

1. Set the Foodi on Sauté mode, add the oil, heat it up, add onions, bay leaves, red bell pepper, garlic, celery, jalapeno, salt and pepper, stir and cook for 10 minutes
2. Add cumin, tomato paste, water, beans and coffee, stir, put the pressure lid on and cook on High for 50 minutes
3. Release the pressure naturally for 10 minutes, add the lime zest and lime juice, stir, divide the soup into bowls, top each serving with sour cream and serve.

Vegetable Stock Recipe

Prep + Cooking Time: 11 minutes, Servings: 6

Ingredients:

- 2 large unpeeled yellow onions; sliced lengthwise in half, root ends removed
- 1 bunch fresh flat leaf parsley; tied with string so it's easy to remove
- 2 medium tomatoes fresh or canned
- 2 unpeeled garlic
- 2 medium carrots; snapped in half
- 2 celery stalks; snapped in half
- 1 tbsp. whole black peppercorns
- 2 bay leaves
- Cold water; as needed

Directions:

1. Add the vegetables, herbs and spices to the Multi-cooker base. Pour in cold water to just cover these ingredients.
2. High pressure for 10 minutes. Lock the lid on the Ninja Foodi Multi-cooker and then cook for 10 minutes.

3. To get 10 minutes' cook time, press *Pressure* button and use the Time Adjustment button to adjust the cook time to 10 minutes
4. Pressure Release Let the pressure to come down naturally for at least 20 to 30 minutes, then quick release any pressure left in the pot.
5. Finish the dish. Carefully strain the contents of the cooker into a stainless steel bowl and let cool to room temperature. Reserve the solids or discard them. Freeze the stock if not using in the next couple of days

Chicken Stock Recipe

Prep + Cooking Time: 1 hour 10 minutes, Servings: 10 cups

Ingredients:

- 2 ½ lb. chicken carcasses
- 2 carrots; diced
- 2 bay leaves
- 4 garlic cloves; crushed
- 1 tsp. whole peppercorn
- 2 celery stalks; diced
- 2 onions keep the outer layers too; diced
- 1 tbsp. apple cider vinegar optional
- 10 cups water
- Your favorite fresh herbs

Directions:

1. Optional step: Brown the chicken carcasses in your Ninja Foodi Multi-cooker with 1 tbsp. of oil. This will slightly elevate the flavors and result in a brown stock. Then, add water to deglaze the pot with 1/2 Cup 100 ml of water
2. Add all ingredients in the Ninja Foodi Multi-cooker.
3. High pressure for 60 minutes. Lock the lid on the Ninja Foodi Multi-cooker and then cook for 60 minutes.
4. To get 60 minutes' cook time, press *Pressure* button and use the Time Adjustment button to adjust the cook time to 60 minutes.
5. Pressure Release. When the time is up, open the cooker with the Natural Release method
6. Finish the dish. Open the lid. Strain the stock through a colander discarding the solids and set aside to cool. Let the stock sit in the fridge until the fat rises to the top and form a layer of gel. Then, skim off the fat on the surface.
7. You can use the stock immediately, keep it in the fridge or freeze it for future use

Herbed Whole Roasted Chicken

Prep + Cooking Time: 50 minutes, Servings: 4

Ingredients:

- 1 whole uncooked chicken 4 ½ - 5 lb.
- 1 tbsp. whole black peppercorns
- 2 tbsp. plus 2 tsp. kosher salt, divided.
- 1/4 cup hot water
- 1/4 cup honey
- Juice of 2 lemons 1/4 cup lemon juice
- 5 sprigs fresh thyme
- 5 cloves garlic, peeled, smashed
- 1 tbsp. canola oil
- 2 tsp. ground black pepper

•

Directions:

1. Rinse chicken and tie legs together with cooking twine
2. In a small bowl, mix together lemon juice, hot water, honey, and 2 tbsp. salt. Pour mixture into the pot. Place whole peppercorns, thyme, and garlic in the pot.
3. Place chicken into the Cook & Crisp basket and place basket in pot. Assemble pressure lid, making sure the pressure release valve is in the SEAL position. Select PRESSURE and set to HIGH. Set time to 22 minutes. Select START/STOP to begin
4. When pressure cooking is complete, allow pressure to naturally release for 5 minutes. After 5 minutes, quick release remaining pressure by moving the pressure release valve to the VENT position. Carefully remove lid when unit has finished releasing pressure
5. Brush chicken with canola oil or spray with cooking spray. Season with salt and pepper.
6. Close crisping lid. Select AIR CRISP, set temperature to 400°F, and set time to 8 minutes. Select START/STOP to begin. Cook until desired level of crispness is reached, adding up to 10 additional minutes
7. Cooking is complete when internal temperature reaches 165°F. Remove chicken from basket using 2 large serving forks. Let rest for 5 to 10 minutes before serving

Chicken and Chimichuri

Prep + Cooking Time: 45 minutes, Servings: 2

Ingredients:

- 2 chicken breasts, bone-in, skin-on
- 1 tbsp. olive oil
- 1 tbsp. fennel, ground
- 1 tbsp. chili powder
- 1 tbsp. sweet paprika
- 1 tsp. garlic powder
- 1 tsp. onion powder
- 1 tsp. cumin, ground
- A pinch of salt and black pepper

For the chimichuri:

- ¼ cup olive oil
- ½ bunch parsley
- 4 garlic cloves; minced.
- 1 shallot; chopped.
- ½ bunch cilantro
- Zest and juice of 1 lemon

Directions:

1. In a bowl mix the paprika with salt, pepper, fennel, chili powder, garlic powder, onion powder, 1 tbsp. oil and the cumin and whisk well
2. Add the chicken breasts and toss them well. Put the basket in the Foodi, add the chicken, set the machine on Air Crisp mode and cook the meat at 375 °F for 35 minutes
3. In a blender, mix the cilantro with ¼ cup oil, parsley, the garlic, shallot, lemon zest and lemon juice and pulse well. Divide the chicken breasts between plates, top with the chimichuri and serve

Cumin Chicken Wings

Prep + Cooking Time: 30 minutes, Servings: 4

Ingredients:

- 8 chicken wings, halved
- ¼ cup chicken stock
- 2 garlic cloves; minced.
- 1 tbsp. olive oil
- 2 tsp. cumin, ground
- Salt and black pepper to the taste

Directions:

1. Put the chicken wings in the Foodi's basket, set the machine on Air Crisp and cook them at 360 °F for 10 minutes and transfer to a bowl
2. Clean the machine, set it on Sauté mode, add the oil and heat it up. Add the chicken wings and all the other ingredients, toss and cook everything for 10 more minutes

Great Chicken Wings

Prep + Cooking Time: 35 minutes, Servings: 4

Ingredients:

- 2 lbs. chicken wings
- 2 tbsp. buffalo sauce
- ½ cup water
- 2 tbsp. canola oil

Directions:

1. Put the water in the Foodi, add the Air Crisp basket and put the wings in the basket. Put the pressure lid on, cook on High for 5 minutes, release the pressure naturally for 10 minutes and toss the wings with the oil
2. Set the machine on Air Crisp mode, cook the wings for 15 minutes more at 390 °F and transfer them to a bowl. Add the buffalo sauce, toss well and serve

Creamy Asparagus Soup

Prep + Cooking Time: 11 minutes, Servings: 4

Ingredients:

- 1 lb. asparagus; tough ends removed, cut into 1-inch pieces
- 3 green onions; sliced crosswise into 1/4-inch pieces
- 1 tbsp. olive oil
- 4 cups salt-free Chicken Stock
- 1 tsp. ground white pepper; plus more as needed
- 1/2 cup heavy cream
- 1 tbsp. unsalted butter
- 1 tbsp. all-purpose flour
- 2 tsp. salt

Directions:

1. Heat the Ninja Foodi Multi-cooker using the *Sauté* function, add the oil, green onions and a pinch of salt. Sauté the green onions for a few minutes, then add the asparagus and stock
2. High pressure for 5 minutes. Lock the lid on the Ninja Foodi Multi-cooker and then cook for 5 minutes.
3. To get 5 minutes' cook time, press *Pressure* button and use the Time Adjustment button to adjust the cook time to 5 minutes.
4. Meanwhile, make a blond roux: In a small saucepan over low heat, mix the butter and flour and cook, constantly stirring, until the butter has melted and the mixture foams and begins to turn golden beige. Remove from the heat.
5. Pressure Release. When the time is up, open the cooker with the Natural Release method
6. Finish the dish. Add the roux, salt and pepper to the soup and puree with an immersion blender until smooth. Taste and season with more pepper if you wish. Swirl in the cream just before serving. Serve and Enjoy!

Chicken and Tomatoes

Prep + Cooking Time: 25 minutes, Servings: 4

Ingredients:

- 2 chicken breasts, skinless, boneless and cubed
- ¼ cup cheddar; grated.
- ½ cup tomatoes; chopped.
- ½ cup heavy cream
- ¾ cup chicken stock
- 2 garlic cloves; minced.
- 2 tbsp. basil; chopped.
- 1 tbsp. olive oil
- 1 tbsp. rosemary; chopped.

- 1 tsp. chili powder
- Salt and black pepper to the taste

Directions:

1. Set the Foodi on Sauté mode, add the oil and heat it up. Add the garlic, tomatoes, rosemary, chili, salt and pepper, stir and cook for 5 minutes
2. Add all the other ingredients, toss, put the pressure lid on and cook on High for 15 minutes. Release the pressure naturally for 10 minutes, divide everything into bowls and serve

Rosemary Turkey

Prep + Cooking Time: 60 minutes, Servings: 4

Ingredients:

- 2 turkey breasts, skinless, boneless and halved
- 1 tbsp. lime juice
- 2 tbsp. olive oil
- 2 tsp. garlic powder
- 1 tsp. rosemary, dried
- Salt and black pepper to the taste

Directions:

1. In a bowl mix all the ingredients and toss. Put the basket in the Foodi machine, put the turkey breasts in it, set the machine on Air Crisp and cook at 370 °F for 35 minutes, flipping the turkey halfway. Serve hot with a side salad

Turkey Breast

Prep + Cooking Time: 1 hour 10 minutes, Servings: 4

Ingredients:

- 1 frozen turkey breast with frozen gravy packet
- 1 whole onion

Directions:

1. Place frozen turkey breast, rozen gravy packet and whole onion in the Ninja Foodi Multi-cooker
2. High pressure for 30 minutes. Lock the lid on the Ninja Foodi Multi-cooker and then cook for 30 minutes.
3. To get 30 minutes' cook time, press *Pressure* button and use the Time Adjustment button to adjust the cook time to 30 minutes
4. Pressure Release. Use natural release method.
5. Remove lid, turn turkey breast over
6. High pressure for 30 minutes. Replace lid on the Ninja Foodi Multi-cooker and then cook for 30 minutes.
7. To get 30 minutes' cook time, press *Pressure* button
8. and use the Time Adjustment button to adjust the cook time to 30 minutes.

9. Pressure Release. Use natural release method, again.
10. Finish the dish. Close crisping lid. Select *Air Crisp*, set temperature to 360°F and set time to 10 minutes. Check after 5 minutes, cooking for an additional 5 minutes if dish needs more browning
11. Remove mesh. Remove turkey and slice. Places slices and turkey gravy into serving dish

Stuffed Chicken Recipe

Prep + Cooking Time: 30 minutes, Servings: 4

Ingredients:

- 4 Chicken Breasts, skinless
- 1 cup Baby Spinach, frozen
- 1/2 cup crumbled Feta Cheese
- 2 tbsp. Olive Oil
- 2 tsp dried Parsley
- 1/2 tsp dried Oregano
- 1/2 tsp Garlic Powder
- Salt and Black Pepper to taste
- 1 cup Water

Directions:

1. Wrap the chicken in plastic and put on a cutting board. Use a rolling pin to pound flat to a quarter inch thickness. Remove the plastic wrap
2. In a bowl, mix spinach, salt, and feta cheese and scoop the mixture onto the chicken breasts. Wrap the chicken to secure the spinach filling in it
3. Use toothpicks to secure the wrap firmly from opening. Gently season the chicken pieces with oregano, parsley, garlic powder, and pepper.
4. Select Sear/Sauté mode on Foodi Ninja. Heat the oil, add the chicken, and sear to golden brown on each side. Work in 2 batches.
5. Remove the chicken onto a plate and set aside. Pour the water into the pot and use a spoon to scrape the bottom of the pot to let loose any chicken pieces or seasoning that is stuck to the bottom of the pot. Fit the reversible rack into the pot with care as the pot will still be hot
6. Transfer the chicken onto the rack. Seal the lid and select Pressure mode on High pressure for 10 minutes. Press Start/Stop.
7. Once the timer has ended, do a quick pressure release. Close the crisping lid and cook on Bake/Roast mode for 5 minutes at 370 F.
8. Plate the chicken and serve with a side of sautéed asparagus, and some slices of tomatoes

Chapter 7 Soup Recipes

Chicken Noodle Soup Recipe

Prep + Cooking Time: 30 minutes, Servings: 6

Ingredients:

- 2 large bone in skinless chicken breasts about 1 lb. each
- 1 medium red onion; halved
- 6 cups chicken broth
- 2 medium carrots
- 2 fresh thyme sprigs
- 2 fresh sage sprigs
- 2 medium garlic cloves; peeled
- 4-ounces wide egg noodles
- 1 tbsp. minced fresh dill fronds
- 2 tbsp. olive oil
- 1/2 tsp. salt

Directions:

1. Heat the oil in the Ninja Foodi Multi-cooker, turned to the sauté function. Add the chicken and brown well on both sides, about 4 minutes in all, turning once.
2. Pour in the broth; add the onion, carrots, salt, thyme, sage and garlic
3. High pressure for 18 minutes. Lock the lid on the Ninja Foodi Multi-cooker and then cook for 18 minutes.
4. To get 18 minutes' cook time, press *Pressure* button and use the Time Adjustment button to adjust the cook time to 18 minutes.
5. Pressure Release. Use the quick release method to return the pot's pressure to normal
6. Unlock and open the cooker. Transfer the chicken to a cutting board. Cool for a few minutes, then debone and chop the meat into bite size bits; set aside
7. Discard the onion, carrots, thyme, sage and garlic from the pot. Stir in the noodles and dill
8. High pressure for 4 minutes. Lock the lid on the Ninja Foodi Multi-cooker and then cook for 4 minutes.
9. To get 4 minutes' cook time, press *pressure* button and use the Time Adjustment button to adjust the cook time to 4 minutes
10. Pressure Release. Use the quick release method to return the pot's pressure to normal
11. Finish the dish. Unlock and open the cooker. Stir in the chopped chicken. Cover loosely and set aside for a couple of minutes to warm through

Beef Stock Recipe

Prep + Cooking Time: 120 minutes, Servings: 6

Ingredients:

- 2 lb beef soup bones
- 1 large onion; quartered, skin on
- 2 tsp. ground pepper
- 1 tsp. ground Himalayan salt
- 2 tbsp. garlic; minced
- 3 tbsp. apple cider vinegar
- 3 large carrots
- 1 bay leaf
- 3 celery sticks
- Handful fresh parsley
- Water

Directions:

1. Ideally, baking the bones at 375°F for 30 minutes prior to pressure cooking them helps draw out the marrow, but if you only have access to your Multi-cooker, it will still get the job done.
2. To start the stock, place the bones, veggies and seasonings into the Ninja Foodi Multi-cooker
3. Pour in the apple cider vinegar and cover with water. The amount of water will vary based on the size and quantities of your vegetables. You can add in extra greens if you want
4. High pressure for 90 minutes. Lock the lid on the Ninja Foodi Multi-cooker and then cook for 90 minutes
5. To get 90 minutes' cook time, press *Pressure* button and use the time adjustment button to adjust the cook time to 90 minutes
6. Pressure Release. Once complete, quick release the pressure valve, allowing the steam to escape

Potato, Carrot and Leek Soup Recipe

Prep + Cooking Time:20 minutes, Servings: 4

Ingredients:

- 1 lb. carrots; coarsely chopped.
- 1 bouquet garni parsley sprigs; bay leaf, a sprig of thyme, tied tightly with string or in cheesecloth
- 1 large potato; peeled and coarsely chopped.
- 1 medium leek; white and pale green parts only, coarsely chopped.
- 1 tbsp. olive oil
- 2 tbsp. unsalted butter
- 2 tsp. salt

- 4 cups salt free Chicken Stock
- Freshly ground black pepper
- 1/4 cup heavy cream
- 1/8 tsp. freshly grated nutmeg
- Fresh thyme sprigs or chopped fresh chives; for serving

Directions:

1. Heat the Ninja Foodi Multi-cooker using the *Sauté* function, add the oil and butter and cook until the butter has melted. Stir in the chopped leeks and salt and sauté, infrequently stirring, until the leeks have softened about 5 minutes
2. Add the carrots and cook, infrequently stirring, until they are golden on one side, about 5 more minutes. Add the potato, stock, pepper to taste and the bouquet garni
3. High pressure for 10 minutes. Lock the lid on Ninja Foodi Multi-cooker and then cook for 10 minutes.
4. To get 10 minutes' cook time, press *Pressure* button and use the Time Adjustment button to adjust the cook time to 10 minutes.
5. Pressure Release When the time is up, open the cooker with the Normal Release method.
6. Finish the dish. Fish out and discard the bouquet garni. Using an immersion blender, puree the soup in the cooker
7. Stir in the cream and nutmeg. Ladle into bowls and dot each serving with a thyme sprig or a few chopped chives

Tomato Soup Recipe

Prep + Cooking Time: 15 minutes, Servings: 2 to 4

Ingredients:

- 1 14.5-ounce can fire roasted tomatoes
- 1 small roasted red bell pepper; cut into chunks about 1/4 cup
- 1/2 cup sliced onion
- 3/4 cup Chicken Stock or low sodium broth
- 1/4 cup dry or medium dry sherry
- 3 tbsp. olive oil
- 1 tbsp. heavy whipping cream optional
- 1 medium garlic clove; sliced or minced
- 1/8 tsp. ground cumin
- 1/8 tsp. freshly ground black pepper
- Kosher salt

Directions:

1. Set the Ninja Foodi Multi-cooker to sauté, heat the olive oil until it shimmers and flows like water. Add the onions and sprinkle with a pinch or two of kosher salt. Cook for about 5

minutes, stirring until the onions just begin to brown. Add the garlic and cook for 1 to 2 minutes more or until fragrant

2. Pour in the sherry and simmer for 1 to 2 minutes or until the sherry is reduced by half, scraping up any browned bits from the bottom of the pan. Add the tomatoes, roasted red bell pepper and Chicken Stock to the Ninja Foodi Multi-cooker.
3. High pressure for 10 minutes. Lock the lid on the Ninja Foodi Multi-cooker and then cook for 10 minutes.
4. To get 10 minutes' cook time, press *Pressure* button and use the Time Adjustment button to adjust the cook time to 10 minutes.
5. Pressure Release. Use the quick release method. Finish the dish. For a smooth soup, blend using an immersion or standard blender. Add the cumin and pepper and adjust the salt, if necessary. If you like a creamier soup, stir in the heavy cream
6. If using a standard blender, be careful. Steam can build up and blow the lid off if the soup is very hot. Hold the lid on with a towel and blend in batches, if necessary; don't fill the jar more than halfway full

Turkey Meatballs in Tomato Sauce

Prep + Cooking Time: 15 minutes, Servings: 4

Ingredients:

- 1 lb. ground turkey
- 1 large egg, at room temperature and beaten in a small bowl
- 1 28-ounce can whole tomatoes, drained and roughly chopped. about 3 ½ cups
- 1 medium yellow onion, chopped.
- 2 medium celery stalks, thinly sliced
- 1/2 cup plain dried breadcrumbs
- 1/4 cup finely grated Parmesan cheese about 1/2-ounce
- 2 tbsp. unsalted butter
- 1/2 cup chicken broth
- 1 tbsp. packed fresh oregano leaves, minced
- 1/4 tsp. grated nutmeg
- 1/4 cup heavy cream
- 1/2 tsp. dried oregano
- 1/2 tsp. dried rosemary
- 1/2 tsp. ground black pepper
- 1/2 tsp. salt

Directions:

1. Mix the ground turkey, egg, breadcrumbs, cheese, oregano, rosemary, pepper and 1/4 tsp. salt in a large bowl until well combined. Form the mixture into 12 balls

2. Melt the butter in the Ninja Foodi Multi-cooker turned to the sauté function. Add the onion and celery; cook, often stirring, until the onion turns translucent, about 3 minutes.
3. Stir in the tomatoes, broth, oregano and the remaining 1/4 tsp. salt. Drop the meatballs into the sauce.
4. High pressure for 10 minutes. Lock the lid on the Ninja Foodi Multi-cooker and then cook for 10 minutes.
5. To get 10 minutes' cook time, press *Pressure* button and use the Time Adjustment button to adjust the cook time to 10 minutes.
6. Pressure Release. Use the quick release method to drop the pot's pressure to normal
7. Finish the dish. Unlock and open the cooker. Turn the Ninja Foodi Multi-cooker to its sauté function.
8. Stir in the cream and nutmeg; simmer, stirring all the while, for 1 minute to reduce the cream a little and blend the flavors

Chicken Strips

Prep + Cooking Time: 25 minutes, Servings: 4

Ingredients:

- 2 chicken breasts, skinless, boneless and cut into strips
- 2 eggs; whisked.
- 1 cup rice flour
- 3 cups cereal, crushed
- A pinch of salt and black pepper

Directions:

1. In a bowl mix the flour with salt and pepper. Put the eggs in a second bowl and the cereal mixed with salt and pepper in a third one
2. Dredge each chicken strip in flour, egg and cereal and place all the pieces in the Foodi's basket
3. Set the machine on Air Crisp and cook at 390 °F for 15 minutes. Divide the strips between plates and serve.

Olive and Lemon Ligurian Chicken

Prep + Cooking Time: 35 minutes, Servings: 6 to 8

Ingredients:

- 3.5-ounce 100g Black Gourmet Salt-Cured Olives Taggiesche, French or Kalamata
- 3 sprigs of Fresh Rosemary two for chopping, one for garnish
- 1 whole chicken, cut into parts or package of bone in chicken pieces, skin removed or not 1/2 cup 125ml dry white wine
- 2 garlic cloves, chopped.
- 2 sprigs of Fresh Sage

- 1/2 bunch of Parsley Leaves and stems
- 3 lemons, juiced about a 3/4 cup or 180ml
- 4 tbsp. extra virgin olive oil
- 1 tsp. sea salt
- 1/4 tsp. pepper
- 1 fresh lemon, for garnish optional

Directions:

1. Prepare the marinade by finely chopping together the garlic, rosemary, sage and parsley. Place them in a container and add the lemon juice, olive oil, salt and pepper. Mix well and set aside
2. Remove the skin from the chicken save it for a chicken stock
3. In the preheated Ninja Foodi Multi-cooker, with the lid off, add a swirl of olive oil and brown the chicken pieces on all sides for about 5 minutes.
4. De-glaze cooker with the white wine until it has almost all evaporated about 3 minutes
5. Add the chicken pieces back in this time being careful with the order. Put all dark meat wings, legs, thighs first and then the chicken breasts on top so that they do not touch the bottom of the Ninja Foodi Multi-cooker.
6. Pour the remaining marinade on top. Don't worry if this does not seem like enough liquid the chicken will also release its juices into the cooker, too
7. High pressure for 10 minutes. Lock the lid on the Ninja Foodi Multi-cooker and then cook for 10 minutes.
8. To get 10 minutes' cook time, press *Pressure* button and adjust the time
9. Pressure Release. When time is up, open the cooker by releasing the pressure using the Quick Release Method.
10. Finish the dish. Close crisping lid. Select *Air Crisp*, set temperature to 390°F and set time to 10 minutes. Check after 5 minutes, cooking for an additional 5 minutes if dish needs more browning
11. Take the chicken pieces out of the cooker and place on a serving platter tightly covered with foil
12. Reduce the cooking liquid in the Ninja Foodi Multi-cooker, if necessary, with the lid off to 1/4 of its amount or until it becomes thick and syrupy.
13. Put all of the chicken pieces back into the Ninja Foodi Multi-cooker to warm up. Mix and spoon the thick glaze onto the chicken pieces and simmer it in the glaze for a few minutes before serving
14. Sprinkle with fresh rosemary, olives and lemon slices. When serving, caution your guests that the olives still have their pits!

Chicken Drumsticks

Prep + Cooking Time: 30 minutes, Servings: 4

Ingredients:

- 10 chicken drumsticks
- 1 cup coconut milk
- ¼ cup cilantro; chopped.
- A bunch of spring onions; chopped.
- 4 garlic cloves; minced.
- 1 tbsp. lime juice
- 2 tbsp. oyster sauce
- 1 tbsp. ginger; grated.
- 1 tsp. Chinese five spice
- 1 tsp. olive oil
- Salt and black pepper to the taste

Directions:

1. In a blender, mix the spring onions with ginger, garlic, oyster sauce, five spice, salt, pepper, oil and coconut milk and pulse well. Put the chicken drumsticks in the Foodi's baking pan and spread the spring onions mix all over
2. Put the reversible rack in the machine, add the baking pan, set the pot on Baking mode and cook at 370 °F for 20 minutes. Divide the chicken mix between plates, sprinkle the cilantro on top, drizzle the lime juice all over and serve

Spicy Chicken

Prep + Cooking Time: 40 minutes, Servings: 6

Ingredients:

- 3 and ½ lbs. chicken breasts
- 1 ¼ cups yellow onion; chopped.
- 1 cup chicken stock
- 1 tbsp. olive oil
- 1 tbsp. lemon juice
- 2 tbsp. green onions; chopped.
- 2 tsp. hot paprika
- 2 tsp. red pepper flakes
- Salt and black pepper to the taste

Directions:

1. Set the Foodi on Sauté mode, add the oil and heat it up. Add the yellow onion, stir and sauté for 2 minutes. Add all the ingredients, toss, put the pressure lid on and cook on High for 18 minutes
2. Release the pressure naturally for 10 minutes, divide everything into bowls and serve. Add the chicken and the stock, toss, simmer for 1 more minute, transfer the pan to your air fryer and cook at 370 °F for 12 minutes. Divide between plates and serve

Pesto Chicken Breasts

Prep + Cooking Time: 40 minutes, Servings: 4

Ingredients:

- 2 chicken breasts, boneless, skinless and halved
- 4 garlic cloves; minced.
- 1 cup parsley; chopped.
- ½ cup olive oil
- ¼ cup red wine
- A pinch of salt and black pepper

Directions:

1. In a blender, mix the parsley with garlic, salt, pepper, oil and wine and pulse well. In the Foodi's baking pan, combine the chicken with the parsley pesto and toss well
2. Put the reversible rack in the Foodi, add the baking pan, set the pot on Baking mode and cook at 370 °F for 30 minutes. Divide everything between plates and serve

Crispy Chicken Thighs with Carrots and Rice Pilaf

Prep + Cooking Time: 25 minutes, Servings: 4

Ingredients:

- 4 uncooked boneless skin-on chicken thighs
- 1 box 6-ounces rice pilaf
- 2 tbsp. honey, warmed
- 1/2 tsp. smoked paprika
- 1 3/4 cups water
- 1 tbsp. butter
- 4 carrots, peeled, cut in half, lengthwise
- 2 tsp. kosher salt, divided.
- 1 tbsp. extra-virgin olive oil
- 2 tsp. poultry spice
- 1/2 tsp. ground cumin

Directions:

1. Place rice pilaf, water, and butter into pot; stir to incorporate
2. Place reversible rack in the pot, making sure rack is in the higher position. Place carrots in center of rack. Arrange chicken thighs, skin side up, around the carrots. Assemble pressure lid, making sure the PRESSURE RELEASE valve is in the SEAL position. Select PRESSURE and set to HIGH. Set time to 4 minutes. Select START/STOP to begin.
3. While chicken and rice are cooking, stir together warm honey, smoked paprika, cumin, and 1 tsp. salt. Set aside

4. When pressure cooking is complete, quick release the pressure by moving the PRESSURE RELEASE valve to the VENT position. Carefully remove lid when unit has finished releasing pressure
5. Brush carrots with seasoned honey. Brush chicken with olive oil, then season evenly with poultry spice and remaining salt.
6. Close crisping lid. Select BROIL and set time to 10 minutes. Select START/STOP to begin. When cooking is complete, serve chicken with carrots and rice

Chicken And Mushrooms Mix

Prep + Cooking Time: 30 minutes, Servings: 4

Ingredients:

- 2 lbs. chicken breasts, skinless, boneless and cubed
- 12 brown mushrooms, halved
- 1 sweet onion; chopped.
- 2 garlic cloves; minced.
- 1 red bell pepper; chopped.
- 2 tbsp. cheddar cheese, shredded
- 2 tbsp. canola oil
- Salt and black pepper to the taste

Directions:

1. Set the Foodi on Sauté mode, add the oil and heat it up. Add the onion, garlic, salt and pepper, toss and sauté for 3-4 minutes
2. Add the chicken pieces, toss and brown for 2-3 minutes more. Add all the other ingredients except the cheese, toss, put the pressure lid on and cook on High for 10 minutes
3. Release the pressure naturally for 10 minutes, divide the chicken and mushrooms mix between plates, sprinkle the cheese on top and serve.

Turmeric Chicken

Prep + Cooking Time: 25 minutes, Servings: 4

Ingredients:

- 2 chicken breasts, skinless, boneless and cubed
- 2 tbsp. canola oil
- 1 tbsp. turmeric powder
- 1 tbsp. lemon juice
- 1 tbsp. ginger; grated.
- 1 tbsp. sweet paprika
- Salt and black pepper to the taste

Directions:

1. Set the Foodi on Sauté mode, add the oil and heat it up. Add the chicken, toss and brown for 4-5 minutes
2. Add the rest of the ingredients, toss, put the pressure lid on and cook on High for 10 minutes. Release the pressure naturally for 10 minutes, divide everything into bowls and serve

Sweet Chipotle Chicken Wings

Prep + Cooking Time: 25 minutes, Servings: 2

Ingredients:

- 3 tbsp. Mexican hot sauce such as Valentina brand
- 1 tsp. minced canned chipotle in adobo sauce
- 1 cup water, for steaming
- 2 tbsp. honey

Directions:

1. If using whole wings, cut off the tips and discard. Cut the wings at the joint into two pieces each the *drumette and the flat.
2. Add the water and insert the steamer basket or trivet. Place the wings on the steamer insert
3. High pressure for 10 minutes. Close the lid and the pressure valve and then cook for 10 minutes.
4. To get 10 minutes' cook time, press *Pressure* button and the time selector
5. Pressure Release. Use the quick release method. Finish the dish. While the wings are cooking, make the sauce. In a large bowl, whisk together the hot sauce, honey and minced chipotle.
6. Close crisping lid. Select *Air Crisp*, set temperature to 390°F and set time to 10 minutes. Select START/STOP to begin. Serve!

Spicy Turkey Chili

Prep + Cooking Time: 60 minutes, Servings: 4

Ingredients:

- 1 lb. ground turkey
- 1/4 cup your favorite hot sauce
- 1 15-ounce can fire roasted diced tomatoes
- 1 15-ounce can kidney beans, including their liquid
- 1 medium yellow onion, diced
- 2 green bell peppers, seeded and diced
- 2 fresh cayenne peppers, chopped. seeds included
- 4 cloves garlic, chopped.
- 1 cup grated Monterey Jack cheese
- 1 tbsp. olive oil
- 1 tsp. ground cumin
- 1/2 tsp. dried oregano leaves

- 1/4 cup chopped cilantro

Directions:

1. Set the Ninja Foodi Multi-cooker to its *Sauté* setting and add the oil. Add the onions, peppers and garlic and sauté until the onions soften and begin to brown, about 10 minutes. Add the cumin and oregano and sauté two more minutes, until aromatic.
2. Add the ground turkey, breaking it up with a spoon or spatula. Sauté until opaque and cooked through, about 5 minutes
3. Add the hot sauce, canned tomatoes and kidney beans and stir to combine
4. High pressure for 45 minutes. Lock the lid on the Ninja Foodi Multi-cooker and then cook for 45 minutes.
5. To get 45 minutes' cook time, press *pressure* button and use the adjust button to adjust the cook time to 45 minutes.
6. Pressure Release. Use natural release method.
7. Finish the dish. Top with grated cheese and cilantro and serve with rice or cornbread, if desired

Delicious Frozen Chicken Dinner

Prep + Cooking Time: 50 minutes, Servings: 2

Ingredients:

- 2 frozen chicken breasts 8 - 10 ounces each
- 2 tbsp. olive oil, divided.
- 1 small onion, peeled, diced
- 3/4 cup chicken stock
- 1 bag 12-ounces green beans, trimmed
- 1 tsp. black pepper, divided.
- 1/4 cup fresh parsley, chopped.
- 1 cup wild rice blend
- 3 tsp. kosher salt, divided.
- 1 tbsp. Moroccan seasoning "Ras el Hanout"
- 1/4 cup honey mustard sauce

Directions:

1. Select SEAR/SAUTÉ and set to HIGH. Allow to preheat for 5 minutes.
2. After 5 minutes, add 1 tbsp. oil and onion. Cook, stirring occasionally, for 3 minutes, until onions are fragrant. Add wild rice, 2 tsp. salt, and Moroccan seasoning. Cook, stirring frequently, until the rice is coated with oil and very shiny. Add chicken stock and stir to incorporate
3. Place frozen chicken breasts on reversible rack, making sure rack is in the higher position. Place rack inside pot over rice mixture.

4. Assemble pressure lid, making sure the PRESSURE RELEASE valve is in the SEAL position. Select PRESSURE and set to HIGH. Set time to 22 minutes. Select START/STOP to begin
5. While chicken and rice are cooking, toss green beans in a bowl with the remaining oil, salt, and pepper
6. When pressure cooking is complete, allow pressure to naturally release for 10 minutes. After 10 minutes, quick release any remaining pressure by turning the PRESSURE RELEASE valve to the VENT position. Carefully remove lid when unit has finished releasing pressure.
7. Lift reversible rack out of the pot. Stir parsley into rice, then add green beans directly on top of the rice
8. Brush chicken breasts on all sides with honey mustard sauce, then return the reversible rack to the pot over rice and green beans. Close crisping lid. Select BROIL and set time to 10 minutes. Select START/STOP to begin.
9. Cooking is complete when internal temperature reaches 165°F. Serve chicken with green beans and rice

Asian Chicken Delight

Prep + Cooking Time: 40 minutes, Servings: 4

Ingredients:

- 2 chicken breasts, skinless, boneless and cubed
- 14 oz. water
- 2 red chilies; chopped.
- 1 bunch spring onions; chopped.
- 1 tbsp. ginger; grated.
- 1 tbsp. rice wine
- 1 tbsp. olive oil
- 1 tbsp. soy sauce
- 1 tsp. sesame oil

Directions:

1. Set the Foodi on Sauté mode, add the olive oil and the sesame seed oil and heat them up. Add the chilies, spring onions and the ginger, stir and cook for 2-3 minutes
2. Add all the other ingredients, toss, put the pressure lid on and cook on High for 25 minutes. Release the pressure naturally for 10 minutes, divide everything into bowls and serve

Turkey Gluten Free Gravy

Prep + Cooking Time: 60 minutes, Servings: 6

Ingredients:

- 1 4 - 5 lb. bone in, skin on turkey breast
- 2 tbsp. ghee or butter use coconut oil for AIP
- 1 medium onion, cut into medium dice
- 1 large carrot, cut into medium dice
- 1 celery rib, cut into medium dice
- 1 garlic clove, peeled and smashed
- 1 ½ cups bone broth preferably from chicken or turkey bones
- Black pepper omit for AIP
- 2 tsp. dried sage
- 1/4 cup dry white wine
- 1 bay leaf
- 1 tbsp. tapioca starch optional
- Salt to taste

Directions:

1. Set the *Sauté* function. Pat turkey breast dry and generously season with salt and pepper. Melt cooking fat in the Ninja Foodi Multi-cooker.
2. Brown turkey breast, skin side down, about 5 minutes and transfer to a plate, leaving fat in the pot
3. Add onion, carrot and celery to pot and cook until softened, about 5 minutes. Stir in garlic and sage and cook until fragrant, about 30 seconds
4. Pour in wine and cook until slightly reduced about 3 minutes. Stir in broth and bay leaf. Using a wooden spoon, scrape up all browned bits stuck on the bottom of pot.
5. Place turkey skin side up in the pot with any accumulated juices.
6. High pressure for 35 minutes. Lock the lid on the Ninja Foodi Multi-cooker and then cook for 35 minutes.
7. To get 35 minutes' cook time, press *Pressure* button and use the Time Adjustment button to adjust the cook time to 35
8. Pressure Release. Use quick release method and carefully remove lid
9. Finish the dish. Close crisping lid. Select *Air Crisp*, set temperature to 375°F and set time to 10 minutes. Check after 5 minutes, cooking for an additional 5 minutes if dish needs more browning.
10. Transfer turkey breast to carving board or plate and tent loosely with foil, allowing it to rest while you prepare the gravy.
11. Use an immersion blender or carefully transfer cooking liquid and vegetables to blender and puree until smooth. Return to heat and cook until thickened and reduced to about 2 cups. Adjust seasoning to taste. Slice turkey breast and serve with hot gravy. Enjoy!

Cheddar Chicken Breast

Prep + Cooking Time: 30 minutes, Servings: 4

Ingredients:

- 16 oz. salsa
- 1 lb. chicken breast, boneless and skinless
- 1 ½ cup cheddar cheese; grated.
- ¼ cup cilantro; chopped.
- 1 tsp. sweet paprika
- 1 tbsp. olive oil
- Salt and black pepper to the taste

Directions:

1. In your Foodi's baking pan, combine all the ingredients except the cheese. Sprinkle the cheese over the chicken
2. Put the reversible rack in the machine, add the baking pan inside, set the pot on Baking mode and cook at 380 °F for 20 minutes. Divide between plates and serve

Chicken Pot Pie Recipe

Prep + Cooking Time: 35 minutes, Servings: 6

Ingredients:

- 2 lb. uncooked boneless skinless chicken breasts, cut in 1-inch cubes
- 1/2 stick 1/4 cup unsalted butter
- 1/2 large onion, peeled, diced
- 1 large carrot, peeled, diced
- 2 cloves garlic, peeled, minced
- 1 stalk celery, diced
- 1/2 cup frozen peas
- 1 ½ tsp. fresh thyme, minced
- 2 tsp. kosher salt
- 1/2 tsp. black pepper
- 1/2 cup heavy cream
- 1 cup chicken broth
- 1 tbsp. fresh Italian parsley, minced
- 1/4 cup all-purpose flour

Directions:

1. Select SEAR/SAUTÉ and set to MD:HI. Select START/STOP to begin. Allow to preheat for 5 minutes. After 5 minutes, add butter to pot. Once it melts, add onion, carrot, and garlic, and SAUTÉ until softened, about 3 minutes

2. Add chicken and broth to the pot. Assemble pressure lid, making sure the PRESSURE RELEASE valve is in the SEAL position. Select PRESSURE and set to HIGH. Set time to 5 minutes. Select START/STOP to begin
3. When pressure cooking is complete, quick release the pressure by moving the PRESSURE RELEASE valve to the VENT position. Carefully remove lid when unit has finished releasing pressure
4. Select SEAR/SAUTÉ and set to MD:HI. Select START/STOP to begin. Add remaining ingredients to pot, except pie crust. Stir until sauce thickens and bubbles, about 3 minutes
5. Lay pie crust evenly on top of the filling mixture, folding over edges if necessary. Make a small cut in center of pie crust so that steam can escape during baking. Close the crisping lid. Select BROIL and set time to 10 minutes. Select START/STOP to begin.
6. When cooking is complete, remove pot from unit and place on a heat-resistant surface. Let rest 10 to 15 minutes before serving

Chicken Casserole

Prep + Cooking Time: 40 minutes, Servings: 4

Ingredients:

- 1 lb. chicken meat, ground
- 12 eggs; whisked.
- 1 cup baby spinach
- ½ tsp. sweet paprika
- 1 tbsp. olive oil
- Salt and black pepper to the taste

Directions:

1. In a bowl mix all the ingredients except the oil and toss them. Put the reversible rack in the Foodi, place the baking pan inside, add the oil and spread
2. Pour the chicken mix in the pan and cook the casserole for 30 minutes on Baking mode at 350 °F. Divide between plates and serve for breakfast.

Cream of Sweet Potato Soup Recipe

Prep + Cooking Time: 11 minutes, Servings: 6

Ingredients:

- 2 lb. sweet potatoes about 2 large; peeled and cut into 2-inch pieces
- 8 tbsp. 1 stick unsalted butter; cut into small pieces
- 1/2 tsp. ground cinnamon
- 1/2 tsp. ground ginger
- 1/4 tsp. baking soda
- 2 ½ cups chicken broth
- 1/2 cup heavy cream

- 1 tsp. salt

Directions:

1. Melt the butter in a Ninja Foodi Multi-cooker turned to the browning function. Stir in the sweet potatoes, salt, cinnamon, ginger and baking soda. Pour 1/2 cup water over everything
2. High pressure for 15 minutes. Lock the lid on the Ninja Foodi Multi-cooker and then cook for 15 minutes.
3. To get 15 minutes' cook time, press *Pressure* button and then adjust the time
4. Pressure Release. Use the quick release method to bring the pot's pressure back to normal
5. Finish the dish. Unlock and open the pot. Stir in the broth and cream. Use an immersion blender to puree the soup in the pot or ladle the soup in batches into a blender, remove the knob from the blender's lid, cover the hole with a clean kitchen towel and blend until smooth

Butternut Squash Soup with Chicken

Prep + Cooking Time: 30 minutes, Servings: 6

Ingredients:

- 1 ½ lb. of fresh baked butternut squash; peeled and cubed
- 1 cup chicken breast; seasoned, cooked and diced
- 1 onion; diced
- 1 garlic clove; minced
- 2 cans chicken broth
- 1 cup orzo; cooked
- 1/2 cup celery; diced
- 1/2 cup carrots; diced
- 2 tbsp. red pepper flakes
- 2 tbsp. dried parsley flakes
- 1 tomato diced
- 3 tbsp. butter
- 1/4 tsp. freshly ground black pepper

Directions:

1. Set the Ninja Foodi Multi-cooker to sauté and melt butter to sauté the onion, garlic clove, celery and carrots
2. Then add the chicken broth, red pepper flakes, dried parsley flakes, black pepper, baked butternut squash and tomato diced to the Ninja Foodi Multi-cooker.
3. High pressure for 15 minutes. Lock the lid on the Ninja Foodi Multi-cooker and then cook for 15 minutes.
4. To get 15 minutes' cook time, press *Pressure* Button
5. Pressure Release. Use the quick release method
6. Blend/puree until mixture is smooth.

7. High pressure for 5 minutes. Then add it back to your Ninja Foodi Multi-cooker along with the chicken breast and orzo and cook for another 5 minutes
8. To get 5 minutes' cook time, press *Pressure* button and adjust the time.
9. Pressure Release. Use the quick release method. Serve with fresh dinner rolls and butter on the side

Tasty Chicken Soup

Prep + Cooking Time: 45 minutes, Servings: 8

Ingredients:

- 3 peeled carrots chopped into similar size as potatoes for even cooking time
- 4 cups of water and chicken concentrate/bullion of your choice to equal 32-ounces – or if you have it, use chicken stock
- 2 frozen boneless skinless chicken breasts
- 4 washed medium size diced potatoes I did not peel you can if you want
- 1/2large onion diced
- Salt and pepper to taste flavors will intensify while under pressure

Directions:

1. Mix the broth, chicken, potatoes, onion, carrots, salt and pepper in the Ninja Foodi Multi-cooker
2. High pressure for 35 minutes. Lock the lid on the Ninja Foodi Multi-cooker and then cook for 35 minutes
3. To get 35 minutes' cook time, press *pressure* button and use the Time Adjustment button to adjust the cook time to 35 minutes
4. Pressure Release Let the pressure to come down naturally for at least 15 minutes, then quick release any pressure left in the pot. Open when all pressure is released stir and enjoy.

Colombian Style Chicken Soup Recipe

Prep + Cooking Time: 20 minutes, Servings: 4

Ingredients:

- 3 bone in chicken breasts about 2 lb. or 907 g
- 5 cups 1.2 L water
- 1 ½ tsp. kosher salt
- 1 ½ lb. Yukon gold potatoes, cut into 1/2-inch 13 mm pieces
- 1 ear corn, cut into 4 pieces
- 1 medium yellow onion, cut in half
- 2 medium carrots, cut in half crosswise
- 2 ribs celery, cut in half crosswise
- 1/4 cup sour cream
- 1 tbsp. capers, rinsed

- 1/4 tsp. freshly ground black pepper
- 1 avocado
- 1 tsp. dried oregano
- 1 lime; quartered
- 8 sprigs fresh cilantro

Directions:

1. To the Ninja Foodi Multi-cooker, add the onion, carrots, celery, chicken, water and salt
2. High pressure for 15 minutes. Lock the lid on the Ninja Foodi Multi-cooker and then cook for 15 minutes.
3. To get 15 minutes' cook time, press *Pressure* Button and then adjust the time
4. Pressure Release. Use the *Quick Release* method to vent the steam, then open the lid. Transfer the chicken to a large bowl. When cool enough to handle, shred into pieces, discarding the skin and bones
5. Discard the onion, carrots and celery. Add the potatoes and corn to the broth.
6. High pressure for 2 minutes. Lock the lid on the Ninja Foodi Multi-cooker and then cook for 2 minutes
7. To get 2 minutes' cook time, press *Pressure* button and use the Time Adjustment button to adjust the cook time to 2 minutes.
8. Pressure Release. Use the *Quick Release* method to vent the steam, then open the lid
9. Finish the dish. Stir in the chicken and pepper.
10. Divide the soup among bowls. Peel, pit and slice the avocado. Top the soup with the avocado, sour cream, capers, oregano and cilantro.
11. Serve with the lime quarters for squeezing

French Onion Soup Recipe

Prep + Cooking Time: 40 minutes, Servings: 4

Ingredients:

- 1-ounce Gruyère or other Swiss-style cheese; coarsely grated about 1/3 cup
- 1/4 cup dry sherry
- 2 cups low sodium chicken broth
- 1/2 cup Beef Stock; Mushroom Stock or low sodium broth
- 4 cups thinly sliced white or yellow onions; divided.
- 2 thin slices French or Italian bread
- 1/2 tsp. kosher salt; plus additional for seasoning
- 1/2 tsp. Worcestershire sauce
- 2 tbsp. unsalted butter; divided.
- 1/4 tsp. dried thyme
- 1 tsp. sherry vinegar or red wine vinegar; plus additional as needed

Directions:

1. Set the Ninja Foodi Multi-cooker to *Sauté*, heat 1 tbsp. of butter until it stops foaming and then add 1 cup of onions. Sprinkle with a pinch or two of kosher salt and stir to coat with the butter. Cook the onions in a single layer for about 4 minutes or until browned
2. Resist the urge to stir them until you see them browning. Stir them to expose the other side to the heat and cook for 4 minutes more. The onions should be quite browned but still slightly firm. Remove the onions from the pan and set aside
3. Pour the sherry into the pot and stir to scrape up the browned bits from the bottom. When the sherry has mostly evaporated, add the remaining 1 tbsp. of butter and let it melt
4. Stir in the remaining 3 cups of onions and sprinkle with 1/2 tsp. of kosher salt
5. High pressure for 25 minutes. Lock the lid on the Ninja Foodi Multi-cooker and then cook for 25 minutes.
6. To get 25 minutes' cook time, press *Pressure* button and use the Time Adjustment button to adjust the cook time to 25 minutes.
7. Pressure Release Use the quick release method. Unlock and remove the lid.
8. The onions should be pale and very soft, with a lot of liquid in the pot. Add the chicken broth, Beef Stock, Worcestershire sauce and thyme
9. High pressure for 10 minutes. Lock the lid on the Ninja Foodi Multi-cooker and then cook for 10 minutes.
10. To get 10 minutes' cook time, press *Pressure* button and use the Time Adjustment button to adjust the cook time to 10 minutes.
11. Pressure Release Use the quick release method
12. Finish the dish. Unlock and remove the lid. Stir in the sherry vinegar and taste. The soup should be balanced between the sweetness of the onions the savory stock and the acid from the vinegar. If it seems bland, add a pinch or two of kosher salt or a little more vinegar
13. Stir in the reserved cup of onions and keep warm while you prepare the cheese toasts
14. Preheat the broiler. Reserve 2 tbsp. of the cheese and sprinkle the remaining cheese evenly over the 2 bread slices. Place the bread slices on a sheet pan under the broiler for 2 to 3 minutes or until the cheese melts
15. Place 1 tbsp. of the reserved cheese in each of 2 bowls. Ladle the soup into the bowls, float a toast slice on top of each and serve.

Chapter 8 Fish & Seafood Recipes

Chili Garlic Black Mussels Recipe

Prep + Cooking Time: 45 minutes, Servings: 4

Ingredients:

- 1 ½ lb. Black Mussels, cleaned and de-bearded
- 3 tbsp. Olive Oil
- 1 White Onion, chopped finely
- 10 Tomatoes, skin removed and chopped.
- 3 large Chilies, seeded and chopped.
- 1 cup Dry White Wine
- 3 cups Vegetable Broth
- 1/3 cup fresh Basil Leaves
- 3 cloves Garlic, peeled and crushed
- 4 tbsp. Tomato Paste
- 1 cup fresh Parsley Leaves

Directions:

1. Heat the olive oil on Sear/Sauté mode, and stir-fry the onion, until soft. Add the chilies and garlic, and cook for 2 minutes, stirring frequently
2. Stir in the tomatoes and tomato paste, and cook for 2 more minutes. Then, pour in the wine and vegetable broth. Let simmer for 5 minutes
3. Add the mussels, close the lid, secure the pressure valve, and press Steam mode on High pressure for 3 minutes. Press Start/Stop to start cooking
4. Once the timer has ended, do a natural pressure release for 15 minutes, then a quick pressure release, and open the lid
5. Remove and discard any unopened mussels. Then, add half of the basil and parsley, and stir. Close the crisping lid and cook on Broil mode for 5 minutes
6. Dish the mussels with sauce in serving bowls and garnish it with the remaining basil and parsley. Serve with a side of crusted bread

Shrimp Bowls

Prep + Cooking Time: 18 minutes, Servings: 4

Ingredients:

- 1 lb. big shrimp, deveined and peeled
- 1 cup tomato puree
- 1 tbsp. sweet paprika
- 1 tbsp. cilantro; chopped.
- Salt and black pepper to the taste

Directions:

1. Set the Foodi on Sauté mode, add the shrimp, toss a bit and cook for 2 minutes. Add the rest of the ingredients, toss, put the pressure lid on and cook on High for 6 more minutes
2. Release the pressure naturally for 10 minutes, divide everything into bowls and serve as an appetizer.

Balsamic Salmon

Prep + Cooking Time: 20 minutes, Servings: 2

Ingredients:

- 2 salmon fillets, boneless
- 1/3 cup balsamic vinegar
- 3 shallots; chopped.
- 2 tbsp. canola oil
- 2 tbsp. lemon juice
- ½ tsp. garlic powder
- Salt and black pepper to the taste

Directions:

1. In a bowl mix all the ingredients and toss. Put the salmon mix in your Foodi's baking pan.
2. Place the reversible rack in the machine, add the baking pan inside, set the Foodi on Baking mode and cook everything at 360 °F for 15 minutes. Divide everything between plates and serve

Creamy Shrimp

Prep + Cooking Time: 20 minutes, Servings: 2

Ingredients:

- 1 lb. shrimp, peeled and deveined
- 2 garlic cloves; minced.
- ½ cup chicken stock
- ¼ cup heavy cream
- 1 tbsp. chives; chopped.
- 1 tbsp. butter, melted
- 1 tbsp. parsley; chopped.
- Salt and black pepper to the taste

Directions:

1. Set the Foodi on Sauté mode, add the butter and heat it up. Add the garlic and the chives, stir and cook for 2 minutes
2. Add the shrimp, cream, salt, pepper, stock and the parsley, toss, put the pressure lid on, set the pot on High and cook the shrimp for 8 minutes. Divide everything into bowls and serve

Special Farro With Fennel and Smoked Trout

Prep + Cooking Time: 50 minutes, Servings: 4

Ingredients:

- 1 cup semi perlato farro
- 12-ounces smoked trout; skinned and chopped.
- 1 large fennel bulb; trimmed and shaved into thin strips
- 1/4 cup regular or low-fat sour cream
- 1/2 cup regular or low-fat mayonnaise
- 3 tbsp. lemon juice
- 1 tsp. sugar
- 2 tbsp. Dijon mustard
- 1 tsp. ground black pepper

Directions:

1. Pour the farro into the Ninja Foodi Multi-cooker; pour in enough water that the grains are submerged by 2 inches
2. High pressure for 17 minutes. Lock the lid on the Ninja Foodi Multi-cooker and then cook for 17 minutes.
3. To get 17 minutes' cook time, press *Pressure* button and use the Time Adjustment button to adjust the cook time to 17 minutes
4. Pressure Release. Use the quick release method to drop the pot's pressure to normal
5. Finish the dish. Unlock and open the cooker. Place the fennel strips in a colander set in the sink and drain the farro into the colander over the fennel. Toss well, then let cool for 30 minutes in the colander
6. Whisk the mayonnaise, sour cream, lemon juice, mustard, sugar and pepper in a large serving bowl until creamy. Add the farro, fennel and smoked trout; toss gently to coat well

Cod Fillets

Prep + Cooking Time: 22 minutes, Servings: 2

Ingredients:

- 2 cod fillets, boneless
- 2 leeks, sliced
- ½ cup pecans; chopped.
- 1 tbsp. olive oil
- Salt and black pepper to the taste

Directions:

1. Set the Foodi on Sauté mode, add the oil and heat it up. Add the leeks, salt and pepper, stir and sauté for 5 minutes

2. Add the fish fillets, season them with salt and pepper, put the pressure lid on and cook on High for 12 minutes. Release the pressure naturally for 10 minutes, divide everything between plates and serve.

Paprika Trout Fillets

Prep + Cooking Time: 22 minutes, Servings: 4

Ingredients:

- 4 trout fillets, boneless
- 1 tbsp. olive oil
- 2 tsp. sweet paprika
- 1 tsp. garlic powder
- ½ tsp. chili powder
- Salt and black pepper to the taste
- Juice of 1 lime

Directions:

1. Grease the Foodi's baking pan with the oil, add the fish and the other ingredients and toss. Put the reversible rack in the machine, add the baking pan, set the pot on Baking mode and cook everything at 370 °F for 12 minutes Divide the fish between plates and serve

Different Shrimp Cocktail

Prep + Cooking Time: 18 minutes, Servings: 4

Ingredients:

- 1 lb. shrimp, peeled and deveined
- 1/3 cup red wine
- 1 tbsp. oregano; chopped.
- 2 tbsp. olive oil

Directions:

1. Set the Foodi on Sauté mode, add the oil, heat it up, add the shrimp, toss and sauté for 2 minutes
2. Add the rest of the ingredients, toss, put the pressure lid on and cook at 370 °F for 6 minutes more. Divide into cups and serve as an appetizer

Crusted Cod

Prep + Cooking Time: 30 minutes, Servings: 4

Ingredients:

- 4 cod fillets, boneless
- 1 bunch asparagus, trimmed
- 1 ½ cups water

- 1 ½ cups quinoa
- 1 cup panko bread crumbs
- ¼ cup parsley; chopped.
- ¼ cup butter, melted
- A pinch of salt and black pepper
- Zest and juice of 2 lemons

Directions:

1. Put the quinoa, water and some salt in the Foodi, put the pressure lid on, cook on High for 4 minutes and release the pressure fast for 5 minutes.
2. In a bowl mix panko with parsley, lemon zest, lemon juice, salt and pepper, stir well and press this on each cod fillet
3. Arrange the asparagus over the quinoa, place the reversible rack in the pot over this mix and place the cod fillets on the rack
4. Set the pot on Baking mode and cook everything for 12 minutes. Divide everything between plates and serve.

Carolina Crab Soup Recipe

Prep + Cooking Time: 45 minutes, Servings: 4

Ingredients:

- 2 lb Crabmeat Lumps
- 2 Celery Stalk, diced
- 1 ½ cup Chicken Broth
- 3/4 cup Heavy Cream
- 6 tbsp. Butter
- 6 tbsp. All-purpose Flour
- Salt to taste
- 1 White Onion, chopped.
- 3 tsp. Worcestershire Sauce
- 3 tsp. Old Bay Seasoning
- 3/4 cup Muscadet
- 3 tsp. minced Garlic
- 1/2 cup Half and Half Cream
- 2 tsp. Hot Sauce
- Lemon Juice, Chopped Dill for serving

Directions:

1. Melt the butter on Sear/Sauté mode, and mix in the all-purpose flour, in a fast motion to make a rue. Add celery, onion, and garlic. Stir and cook until soft and crispy, for 3 minutes
2. While stirring, gradually add the half and half cream, heavy cream, and broth

3. Let simmer for 2 minutes. Add Worcestershire sauce, old bay seasoning, Muscadet, and hot sauce.
4. Stir and let simmer for 15 minutes. Add the crabmeat and mix it well into the sauce
5. Close the crisping lid and cook on Broil mode for 10 minutes to soften the meat. Dish into serving bowls, garnish with dill and drizzle squirts of lemon juice over
6. Serve with a side of garlic crusted bread

Flavored Salmon

Prep + Cooking Time: 20 minutes, Servings: 4

Ingredients:

- 1 jalapeno pepper; chopped.
- 4 salmon fillets, boneless
- 3 garlic cloves; minced.
- 1 small red onion; chopped.
- ½ cup cilantro; chopped.
- 1/3 cup canola oil
- 1 tsp. red pepper flakes
- 3 tbsp. balsamic vinegar
- 2 tbsp. parsley; chopped.
- 2 tbsp. basil; chopped.
- Salt and black pepper to the taste

Directions:

1. In the Foodi's baking pan, combine all the ingredients and toss them. Put the reversible rack in the Foodi, add the baking pan, set the pot on Baking mode and cook everything at 360 °F for 10 minutes. Divide the fish between plates and serve.

Squash Curry

Prep + Cooking Time: 45 minutes, Servings: 6

Ingredients:

- 28 oz. firm tofu; drained. and cubed
- 2 yellow onions, sliced
- A pinch of salt and black pepper
- 6 garlic cloves; minced.
- 2 cups coconut milk
- 2 cups butternut squash; cubed.
- ¼ cup cilantro; chopped.
- 2 tbsp. peanut butter, soft
- 2 tbsp. olive oil

- 2 tsp. curry powder
- 2 tsp. fish sauce
- Juice of 1 lime

Directions:

1. Set the Foodi on Sauté mode, add the oil, heat it up, add the tofu, cook for 2 minutes on each side and transfer to a bowl. Add the squash, onions, salt and pepper to the machine and sauté everything for 2 more minutes.
2. Add the garlic, fish sauce, coconut milk, peanut butter and the curry powder, stir and cook everything for 2 minutes
3. Add the lime juice, return the tofu, put the pressure lid on and cook everything on Low for 20 minutes. Add the lime juice and the cilantro, toss, divide everything into bowls and serve.

Shrimp And Peppers

Prep + Cooking Time: 23 minutes, Servings: 4

Ingredients:

- 1 lb. shrimp, peeled and deveined
- ½ cup yellow onion; chopped.
- 2 cup red bell pepper, cut into strips
- 1 tbsp. olive oil
- 1 tsp. sweet paprika
- 1 tsp. soy sauce
- Salt and black pepper to the taste

Directions:

1. Set the Foodi on Sauté mode, add the oil and heat it up. Add the onion and the bell peppers, stir and sauté for 5 minutes. Add the soy sauce, salt, pepper and the paprika and toss
2. Add the shrimp, toss, put the pressure lid on and cook on High for 8 minutes Release the pressure fast for 5 minutes, divide the shrimp mix between plates and serve.

Tasty Skewers

Prep + Cooking Time: 13 minutes, Servings: 2

Ingredients:

- 8 shrimps, peeled and deveined
- 8 green bell pepper slices
- 4 garlic cloves; minced.
- 1 tbsp. olive oil
- 1 tbsp. cilantro; chopped.
- Salt and black pepper to the taste

Directions:

1. In a bowl mix the shrimp with the oil, garlic, salt, pepper, cilantro and bell pepper slices and toss. Thread the shrimp and bell pepper slices on skewers and put them all in the Foodi's basket
2. Place the basket in the machine, set it on Air Crisp and cook at 350 °F for 8 minutes. Divide the shrimp skewers between plates and serve

Cod And Green Beans

Prep + Cooking Time: 22 minutes, Servings: 4

Ingredients:

- 4 cod fillets, boneless
- 2 garlic cloves; minced.
- 2 cups green beans, trimmed and halved
- 2 tbsp. cilantro; chopped.
- 4 tbsp. chicken stock
- 1 tbsp. olive oil
- ½ tsp. basil, dried
- ½ tsp. sweet paprika
- Salt and pepper to the taste

Directions:

1. Set the Foodi on Sauté mode, add the oil and heat it up. Add the garlic, basil, paprika, salt and pepper, stir and cook for 2 minutes
2. Add the fish, green beans and the stock, toss, put the pressure lid on and cook on High for 10 minutes. Release the pressure naturally for 10 minutes, add the cilantro, toss, divide everything between plates and serve

Orange Cod Bites

Prep + Cooking Time: 22 minutes, Servings: 4

Ingredients:

- 4 cod fillets, boneless and cubed
- ¼ cup balsamic vinegar
- ¼ cup orange juice
- ½ tbsp. olive oil
- A pinch of salt and black pepper
- Juice of ½ lime

Directions:

1. Set the Foodi on Sauté mode, add the oil and heat it up. Add the cod bites and cook for 2 minutes. Add all the other ingredients, toss, put the pressure lid on and cook on High for 10 minutes
2. Release the pressure naturally for 10 minutes, divide everything into bowls and serve

Chili Cod

Prep + Cooking Time: 20 minutes, Servings: 2

Ingredients:

- 2 cod fillets, boneless
- 3 red chili pepper; chopped.
- 2 tbsp. olive oil
- 2 tbsp. garlic; minced.
- 2 tbsp. lime juice
- Salt and black pepper to the taste

Directions:

1. In a bowl combine all the ingredients and toss. Put the fish in the Foodi's basket and insert it in the machine.
2. Set the Foodi on Air Crisp and cook at 370 °F for 10 minutes. Divide between plates and serve right away

Alaskan Cod with Pinto Beans

Prep + Cooking Time: 30 minutes, Servings: 4

Ingredients:

- 2 18 oz Alaskan Cod, cut into 4 pieces each
- 2 cloves Garlic, minced
- 1/2 cup Olive Brine
- 3 cups Chicken Broth
- Salt and Black Pepper to taste
- 2 small Onions, chopped.
- 1 head Fennel, quartered
- 1 cup Pinto Beans, soaked, drained and rinsed
- 1 cup Green Olives, pitted and crushed
- 1/2 cup Basil Leaves
- 1/2 cup Tomato Puree
- 4 tbsp. Olive Oil
- Lemon Slices to garnish

Directions:

1. Heat the olive oil and add the garlic and onion. Stir-fry on Sear/Sauté mode until the onion softens. Pour in chicken broth and tomato puree. Let simmer for about 3 minutes
2. Add fennel, olives, beans, salt, and pepper. Seal the lid and select Steam mode on High pressure for 10 minutes. Press Start/Stop to start cooking.

3. Once the timer has stopped, do a quick pressure release, and open the lid. Transfer the beans to a plate with a slotted spoon. Adjust broth's taste with salt and pepper and add the cod pieces to the cooker.
4. Close the lid again, secure the pressure valve, and select Steam mode on Low pressure for 3 minutes. Press Start/Stop.
5. Once the timer has ended, do a quick pressure release, and open the lid.
6. Remove the cod into soup plates, top with the beans and basil leaves, and spoon the broth over them. Serve with a side of crusted bread

Mustard Salmon Fillets

Prep + Cooking Time: 15 minutes, Servings: 2

Ingredients:

- 2 salmon fillets, boneless
- 1 tbsp. olive oil
- 2 tbsp. mustard
- Salt and black pepper to the taste

Directions:

1. Put the salmon in the Foodi's baking pan. Brush the fillets with mustard and oil and season with salt and pepper
2. Put the reversible rack in the Foodi, add the baking pan inside, set the pot on Baking mode and cook at 370 °F for 10 minutes. Serve with a side salad

Salmon with Bok Choy

Prep + Cooking Time: 15 minutes, Servings: 4

Ingredients:

- 4 frozen skinless salmon fillets 4-ounces, 1-inch thick each
- 1 cup jasmine rice, rinsed
- 3/4 cup water
- 2 heads baby bok choy, stems on, rinsed, cut in half
- 1/4 cup mirin
- 1 tsp. sesame oil
- 1 tsp. kosher salt
- 2 tbsp. red miso paste
- 2 tbsp. butter, softened
- Sesame seeds, for garnish

Directions:

1. Place rice and water into the pot. Stir to combine. Place reversible rack in pot, making sure rack is in the higher position

2. Season salmon with salt, then place on rack. Assemble pressure lid, making sure the PRESSURE RELEASE valve is in the SEAL position. Select PRESSURE and set to HIGH. Set time to 2 minutes. Select START/STOP to begin
3. While salmon and rice are cooking, stir together miso and butter to form a paste. Toss bok choy with mirin and sesame oil
4. When pressure cooking is complete, quick release the pressure by moving the PRESSURE RELEASE valve to the VENT position. Carefully remove lid when unit has finished releasing pressure
5. Gently pat salmon dry with paper towel, then spread miso butter evenly on top of the fillets. Add bok choy to the rack. Close crisping lid. Select BROIL and set time to 7 minutes. Select START/STOP to begin, checking for doneness after 5 minutes
6. When cooking is complete, remove salmon from rack and serve with bok choy and rice. Garnish with sesame seeds, if desired

Tomatillo and Shrimp Casserole

Prep + Cooking Time: 30 minutes, Servings: 4

Ingredients:

- 1 ½ lb. medium shrimp about 30 per pound; peeled and deveined
- 1/4 cup loosely packed fresh cilantro leaves; chopped.
- 1 ½ lb. fresh tomatillos; husked and chopped.
- 1/2 cup bottled clam juice
- 1 cup shredded Monterey jack cheese about 4-ounces
- 2 tbsp. olive oil
- 1 medium yellow onion; chopped.
- 1 small fresh jalapeño chile; stemmed; seeded and minced
- 2 tsp. minced garlic
- 2 tbsp. fresh lime juice

Directions:

1. Heat the oil in the Ninja Foodi Multi-cooker turned to the *Browning* function. Add the onion and cook, often stirring, until translucent, about 3 minutes
2. Add the jalapeño and garlic; cook until aromatic, stirring all the while, less than a minute.
3. Stir in the tomatillos, clam juice and lime juice
4. High pressure for 9 minutes. Lock the lid on the Ninja Foodi Multi-cooker and then cook for 9 minutes.
5. To get 9 minutes' cook time, press *Pressure* button and use the Time Adjustment button to adjust the cook time to 9 minutes.
6. Pressure Release Use the quick release method
7. Finish the dish. Unlock and open the pot. Turn the Ninja Foodi Multi-cooker to its *Sauté* function. Stir in the shrimp and cilantro; cook for 2 minutes, stirring frequently

8. Sprinkle the cheese over the top of the casserole. Close crisping lid and select Broil, set time to 5 minutes. Press Start/Stop button to begin. Serve and enjoy

Lime Cod Fillets

Prep + Cooking Time: 22 minutes, Servings: 4

Ingredients:

- 4 cod fillets, boneless
- 6 tbsp. butter, melted
- 2 tbsp. olive oil
- 3 tbsp. chives; chopped.
- 2 tsp. lime juice
- 3 tsp. lime zest; grated.
- Salt and black pepper to the taste

Directions:

1. Set the Foodi on Sauté mode, add the oil and the butter and heat them up. Add 3 tbsps. chives, lime zest, lime juice, salt and pepper, whisk everything and cook for 3 minutes
2. Add the fish, put the pressure lid on and cook on High for 8 minutes. Release the pressure naturally for 10 minutes, divide everything between plates and serve.

Chapter 9 Side Dish Recipes

Turmeric Cauliflower

Prep + Cooking Time: 30 minutes, Servings: 4

Ingredients:

- 2 cups cauliflower florets
- 1 cup veggie stock
- 1 handful cilantro; chopped.
- 2 garlic cloves; minced.
- 2 tbsp. olive oil
- 2 tsp. turmeric powder
- Salt and black pepper to the taste

Directions:

1. Set the Foodi on Sauté mode, add the oil, heat it up, add the garlic and cook for 1 minute. Add all the ingredients except the cilantro, toss, set the machine on Baking mode and cook at 380 °F for 20 minutes.
2. Add the cilantro, toss divide everything between plates and serve as a side dish

Cauliflower Mix

Prep + Cooking Time: 20 minutes, Servings: 4

Ingredients:

- 1 ½ cup white cauliflower, florets separated
- 1 ½ cups purple cauliflower, florets separated
- 2 garlic cloves; minced.
- ½ cup peas
- 1 carrot; cubed.
- 2 spring onions; chopped.
- 2 and ½ tbsp. soy sauce
- 2 tbsp. olive oil
- A pinch of salt and black pepper

Directions:

1. Set the Foodi on Sauté mode, add the oil and heat it up. Add the spring onions and garlic, stir and cook for 2-3 minutes
2. Add the carrots, all the cauliflower, soy sauce, salt, pepper and the peas, toss, put the pressure lid on and cook on High for 8 minutes. Release the pressure naturally for 10 minutes, divide everything between plates and serve as a side dish

Potato Salad

Prep + Cooking Time: 25 minutes, Servings: 6

Ingredients:

- 2 lbs. red potatoes, scrubbed
- 1 yellow onion; chopped.
- 5 bacon strips; chopped.
- 2 celery stalks; chopped.
- ¼ cup apple cider vinegar
- 1 cup sauerkraut
- ½ cup scallions; chopped.
- ½ cup water
- 1 tbsp. mustard
- ¼ tsp. sweet paprika
- 1 tsp. sugar
- A pinch of salt and black pepper

Directions:

1. Put the potatoes and the water in your Foodi, put the pressure lid on and cook on High for 5 minutes and release the pressure naturally for 10 minutes
2. Cool down the potatoes, peel and cut into cubes. Clean the Foodi, set it on Sauté mode, add the bacon, stir and cook for 5 minutes
3. Add the onion, stir and cook for another 5 minutes. Add the vinegar, toss and cook for 1 more minute.
4. Add the potatoes and all the other ingredients, toss, cook for a couple more minutes, divide everything between plates and serve as a side dish.

Zucchini Spaghetti

Prep + Cooking Time: 10 minutes, Servings: 4

Ingredients:

- 3 zucchinis, cut with a spiralizer
- 1 cup sweet peas
- 1 cup cherry tomatoes, halved
- 6 basil leaves, torn
- 1 tbsp. olive oil
- A pinch of salt and black pepper

For the pesto:

- 1/3 cup pine nuts
- ¼ cup parmesan; grated.
- ½ cup olive oil

- 3 cups basil leaves
- 2 garlic cloves
- A pinch of salt and black pepper

Directions:

1. In a blender, mix ½ cup oil with 3 cups basil, garlic, pine nuts, parmesan, salt and pepper and pulse well. Set the Foodi on Sauté mode, add 1 tbsp. oil and heat it up
2. Add the zucchini spaghetti, peas, tomatoes and the pesto, toss, put the pressure lid on and cook on High for 5 minutes. Release the pressure fast for 5 minutes, add the torn basil leaves, toss, divide everything between plates and serve as a side dish

Garlicky Broccoli

Prep + Cooking Time: 30 minutes, Servings: 4

Ingredients:

- 1 broccoli head, florets separated
- 3 garlic cloves; minced.
- 2 tbsp. lemon juice
- 2 tbsp. parsley; chopped.
- 1 tbsp. olive oil

Directions:

1. Set the Foodi on Sauté mode, add the oil and heat it up. Add the garlic, broccoli and lemon juice, toss and cook for 2 minutes
2. Put the pressure lid on, set the machine on High and cook for 15 minutes. Release the pressure naturally for 10 minutes, divide between plates and serve as a side dish.

Garlic Brussels Sprouts

Prep + Cooking Time: 22 minutes, Servings: 4

Ingredients:

- 1 lb. Brussels sprouts, trimmed and halved
- 2 tbsp. garlic; minced.
- 6 tsp. olive oil
- Salt and black pepper to the taste

Directions:

1. In your Foodi's Air Crisp basket, combine all the ingredients. Put the basket in the pot, set it on Air Crisp mode and cook the sprouts at 400 °F for 12 minutes. Divide between plates and serve as a side dish

Easy Gnocchi

Prep + Cooking Time: 32 minutes, Servings: 6

Ingredients:

- 50 oz. potato gnocchi
- 10 oz. baby spinach
- ½ cup goat cheese, crumbled
- ¼ cup parmesan; grated.
- 1/3 cup white flour
- 3 and ½ cups heavy cream
- 1 ½ cups chicken stock
- A pinch of salt and black pepper

Directions:

1. Set the Foodi on Sauté mode, heat it up, add the stock, cream, flour, salt, pepper and the nutmeg, whisk well and cook for 8 minutes
2. Add the spinach and the gnocchi, sprinkle the parmesan and the goat cheese on top, set the Foodi on Bake mode and cook at 325 °F for 15 minutes. Divide the gnocchi between plates and serve

Warm Potato Salad

Prep + Cooking Time: 30 minutes, Servings: 4

Ingredients:

- 2 gold potatoes, cut into wedges
- 3 tbsp. heavy cream
- 1 tbsp. canola oil
- Salt and black pepper to the taste

Directions:

1. Put the potatoes in the Air Crisp basket and place it in the Foodi. Set the machine on Air Crisp mode and cook at 400 °F for 10 minutes
2. Clean the pot and transfer the potatoes to a bowl. Set the Foodi on Sauté mode, add the oil and heat it up. Add potato wedges, salt, pepper and the heavy cream, toss, cook for 10 minutes more, divide between plates and serve as a side dish

Baby Carrots

Prep + Cooking Time: 25 minutes, Servings: 4

Ingredients:

- 1 lb. baby carrots, trimmed
- 2 tbsp. lime juice
- 2 tsp. olive oil

- 1 tsp. herbs de Provence

Directions:

1. In a bowl mix all the ingredients and toss them. Put the basket in the Foodi, put the carrots in the basket, set the machine on Air Crisp and cook at 350 °F for 15 minutes. Divide between plates and serve as a side dish

Zucchini Fries

Prep + Cooking Time: 22 minutes, Servings: 4

Ingredients:

- 2 small zucchinis, cut into fries
- 2 eggs; whisked.
- 1 cup bread crumbs
- ½ cup white flour
- Cooking spray
- Salt and black pepper to the taste

Directions:

1. In a bowl mix the flour with salt and pepper and stir. Put breadcrumbs in another bowl and the eggs one. Dredge the zucchini fries in flour, eggs and bread crumbs and put them in the Foodi's Air Crisp basket
2. Put the basket in the machine, grease the fries with the cooking spray, set the Foodi on Air Crisp and cook at 400 °F for 12 minutes. Divide the fries between plates and serve as a side dish.

Herbed Sweet Potatoes

Prep + Cooking Time: 25 minutes, Servings: 6

Ingredients:

- 3 lbs. sweet potatoes, cut into wedges
- ½ cup parmesan; grated.
- 2 garlic cloves
- 2 tbsp. butter, melted
- ½ tsp. parsley, dried
- ¼ tsp. sage, dried
- ½ tsp. rosemary, dried
- Salt and black pepper to the taste

Directions:

1. In the Foodi' baking dish, combine all the ingredients and toss. Put the reversible rack in the Foodi, add the baking dish inside, set the machine on Baking mode and cook at 360 °F for 20 minutes
2. Divide the sweet potatoes between plates and serve as a side dish.

Veggie Side Salad

Prep + Cooking Time: 22 minutes, Servings: 4

Ingredients:

- 1 eggplant; cubed.
- 1 green bell pepper; chopped.
- 1 bunch cilantro; chopped.
- 2 garlic cloves; minced.
- 1 yellow onion; chopped.
- 1 tbsp. tomato sauce
- 1 tbsp. olive oil
- Salt and black pepper to the taste

Directions:

1. Set the Foodi on Sauté mode, add the oil and heat it up. Add all the ingredients except the cilantro, toss, put the pressure lid on and cook on High for 12 minutes
2. Release the pressure naturally for 10 minutes, divide between plates and serve as a side dish.

Buttery Broccoli

Prep + Cooking Time: 35 minutes, Servings: 4

Ingredients:

- 1 broccoli head, florets separated
- ½ cup chicken stock
- ½ cup parmesan; grated.
- 2 garlic cloves; minced.
- 1 yellow onion; chopped.
- 2 tbsp. parsley; chopped.
- 3 tbsp. butter
- Salt and black pepper to the taste

Directions:

1. Set the Foodi on Sauté mode, add the butter and melt it. Add the onion and the garlic, stir and cook for 5 minutes
2. Add all the other ingredients except the parsley and the parmesan, toss, set the machine on Baking mode and cook at 360 °F for 20 minutes. Sprinkle the cheese and the parmesan on top, toss, divide between plates and serve as a side dish

Sumac Eggplant

Prep + Cooking Time: 25 minutes, Servings: 6

Ingredients:

- 2 lbs. eggplant; cubed.
- 1 tbsp. olive oil
- 1 tsp. sumac
- 1 tsp. garlic powder
- Juice of 1 lime

Directions:

1. Set the Foodi on Sauté mode, add the oil and heat it up. Add the eggplant, garlic powder, sumac and lime juice, toss, put the pressure lid on and cook on High for 15 minutes
2. Release the pressure naturally for 10 minutes, divide the eggplant mix between plates and serve as a side dish.

Thyme Red Potatoes

Prep + Cooking Time: 40 minutes, Servings: 4

Ingredients:

- 4 red potatoes, thinly sliced
- 1 tbsp. olive oil
- 2 tsp. thyme; chopped.
- Salt and black pepper the taste

Directions:

1. In a bowl mix all the ingredients, toss them and transfer to the Air Crisp basket.
2. Put the basket in the Foodi, set the machine on Air Crisp and cook at 370 °F for 30 minutes. Divide the potatoes between plates and serve as a side dish

Buttery Mushrooms

Prep + Cooking Time: 20 minutes, Servings: 4

Ingredients:

- 1 lb. button mushrooms, halved
- 3 tbsp. butter, melted
- 2 tbsp. parmesan; grated.
- 1 tsp. Italian seasoning
- A pinch of salt and black pepper

Directions:

1. Set the Foodi on Sauté mode, add the butter and heat it up. Add the mushrooms and all the other ingredients, toss, put the pressure lid on and cook on High for 10 minutes

2. Release the pressure naturally for 10 minutes, divide everything between plates and serve as a side dish.

Cauliflower And Pineapple Salad

Prep + Cooking Time: 30 minutes, Servings: 6

Ingredients:

- 2 cauliflower florets
- 1 pineapple, peeled and cubed
- 1 mango, peeled and cubed
- 1 cup chicken stock, heated up
- 2 tsp. olive oil
- Salt and black pepper to the taste

Directions:

1. Set the Foodi on Sauté mode, add the oil, heat it up, add the cauliflower and cook for 5 minutes
2. Add all the other ingredients, put the pressure lid on, cook on High for 15 minutes and release the pressure naturally for 10 minutes. Divide between plates and serve as a side dish.

Squash Mash

Prep + Cooking Time: 30 minutes, Servings: 4

Ingredients:

- 1 cup veggie stock
- 2 tbsp. butter, melted
- 2 tbsp. sour cream
- 1 butternut squash, peeled and cubed
- Salt and black pepper to the taste

Directions:

1. In your Foodi, mix the squash with the stock, salt and pepper, toss, put the pressure lid on and cook on High for 20 minutes
2. Release the pressure naturally for 10 minutes, mash the squash well, add the butter and the sour cream, whisk well, divide between plates and serve as a side dish

Hazelnut Cauliflower Rice

Prep + Cooking Time: 32 minutes, Servings: 4

Ingredients:

- 1 spring onion; chopped.
- 2 garlic cloves; minced.
- 2 cups cauliflower rice

- 2 cups chicken stock
- ½ cup hazelnuts, toasted and chopped
- 1 tbsp. cilantro; chopped.
- 1 tsp. olive oil
- Salt and black pepper to the taste

Directions:

1. Set the Foodi on Sauté mode, add the oil and heat it up. Add the onion and the garlic, stir and cook for 2-3 minutes. Add the cauliflower rice, stock, hazelnuts, salt and pepper, toss, put the pressure lid on and cook on High for 20 minutes
2. Release the pressure naturally for 10 minutes, add the cilantro, toss, divide between plates and serve as a side dish.

Maple Carrots

Prep + Cooking Time: 25 minutes, Servings: 6

Ingredients:

- 2 lbs. carrots, roughly cubed
- 1 tbsp. canola oil
- 2 tbsp. maple syrup
- 1 tbsp. parsley; chopped.

Directions:

1. In a bowl mix all the ingredients and transfer to your Air Crisp basket
2. Put the basket in the Foodi, set the machine on Air Crisp and cook at 350 °F for 20 minutes. Divide between plates and serve as a side dish.

Red Cabbage

Prep + Cooking Time: 30 minutes, Servings: 2

Ingredients:

- 1 red cabbage head, shredded
- 1 cup sour cream
- 1 red onion; chopped.
- 4 bacon slices; chopped.
- Salt and black pepper to the taste

Directions:

1. Set the Foodi on Sauté mode, add the bacon, stir and brown for 3-4 minutes. Add the onion, cabbage, salt and pepper, stir and cook for 4 more minutes
2. Add the sour cream, toss well, put the pressure lid on and cook on High for 12 minutes. Release the pressure naturally for 10 minutes, divide the mix between plates and serve as a side dish.

Green Beans Salad

Prep + Cooking Time: 30 minutes, Servings: 4

Ingredients:

- 1 ½ lbs. green beans, trimmed
- ½ lb. shallots; chopped.
- ¼ cup walnuts; chopped.
- 2 tbsp. olive oil
- Salt and black pepper to the taste

Directions:

1. In your Foodi's Air Crisp basket, combine all the ingredients. Put the basket in the pot, set it on Air Crisp mode and cook at 360 °F for 20 minutes. Divide between plates and serve as a side dish

Roasted Tomato Salad

Prep + Cooking Time: 16 minutes, Servings: 2

Ingredients:

- 20 oz. cherry tomatoes, cut into quarters
- ½ cup cilantro
- 1 white onion, roughly chopped
- 1 jalapeno pepper; chopped.
- Juice of 1 lime
- 1 tbsp. olive oil
- Salt and black pepper to the taste

Directions:

1. Set the Foodi on Sauté mode, add the oil, heat it up, add the onion, stir and sauté for 2-3 minutes.
2. Add all the other ingredients, toss, set the machine on Roast mode and cook at 380 °F for 4 minutes. Divide the tomatoes mix between plates and serve

Mexican Beans

Prep + Cooking Time: 30 minutes, Servings: 4

Ingredients:

- 1 cup canned garbanzo beans; drained.
- 1 cup canned cranberry beans; drained.
- 1 cup chicken stock
- 1 bunch parsley; chopped.
- 1 small red onion; chopped.
- 1 garlic clove; minced.

- 2 celery stalks; chopped.
- 5 tbsp. apple cider vinegar
- 4 tbsp. olive oil
- Salt and black pepper to the taste

Directions:

1. Set the Foodi on Sauté mode, add the oil, heat it up, add the onion and the garlic, stir and sauté for 5 minutes.
2. Add all the other ingredients, toss, put the pressure lid on, cook on High for 15 minutes, release the pressure naturally. Divide between plates and serve as a side dish

Potato Mash

Prep + Cooking Time: 20 minutes, Servings: 4

Ingredients:

- 3 gold potatoes, peeled and cubed
- ½ cup cheddar cheese, shredded
- 1 cup heavy cream
- 1 cup water
- ¼ cup butter, melted
- A pinch of salt and black pepper

Directions:

1. Put the potatoes and the water in the Foodi, put the pressure lid on, cook on High for 10 minutes and release the pressure naturally for 10 minutes. Drain the potatoes, transfer them to a bowl, mash them, add the butter, the cheese, cream, salt and pepper, whisk well, divide between plates and serve as a side dish

Spiced Squash

Prep + Cooking Time: 25 minutes, Servings: 4

Ingredients:

- 6 oz. squash; cubed.
- 2 oz. heavy cream
- 1 small yellow onion; chopped.
- 2 garlic cloves; minced.
- 2 tbsp. olive oil
- ½ tsp. cinnamon powder
- ½ tsp. allspice
- ½ tsp. nutmeg, ground
- ½ tsp. ginger; grated.

Directions:

1. Set the Foodi on Sauté mode, add the oil and heat it up. Add the onion and the garlic, stir and cook for 5 minutes
2. Add all the other ingredients, toss, set the machine on Baking mode and cook everything at 360 °F for 15 minutes. Divide between plates and serve as a side dish.

Beans And Tomatoes Mix

Prep + Cooking Time: 30 minutes, Servings: 6

Ingredients:

- 1 lb. canned red kidney beans; drained..
- ½ lb. cherry tomatoes, cut into quarters.
- 1 yellow onion; chopped.
- 4 garlic cloves; chopped.
- 2 spring onions; minced.
- 1 tsp. olive oil
- 2 tbsp. cilantro; minced.
- 2 tbsp. tomato sauce
- Salt and black pepper to the taste

Directions:

1. In your Foodi's baking pan, combine all the ingredients except the cilantro and toss
2. Put the reversible rack in the machine, add the baking pan inside, set the Foodi on Baking mode and cook everything for 20 minutes. Add the cilantro, stir, divide between plates and serve.

Potatoes and Tomatoes

Prep + Cooking Time: 25 minutes, Servings: 6

Ingredients:

- 15 oz. potatoes; cubed.
- 6 oz. canned tomatoes; chopped.
- 2 spring onions; chopped.
- 2 tbsp. olive oil
- ½ tsp. nutmeg, ground
- Salt and black pepper to the taste

Directions:

1. Set the Foodi on Sauté mode, add the oil, heat it up, add the onions, stir and cook for 2-3 minutes.
2. Add the potatoes, nutmeg, tomatoes, salt and pepper, toss, put the pressure lid on and cook on High for 15 minutes. Release the pressure naturally for 10 minutes, divide the mix between plates and serve as a side dish

Creamy Cauliflower

Prep + Cooking Time: 25 minutes, Servings: 4

Ingredients:

- 1 cauliflower head, florets separated
- ½ cup Italian bread crumbs
- ¼ cup raisins
- ½ cup heavy cream
- ½ cup parmesan; grated.
- 1 cup beer
- 1 tbsp. white flour
- 1 tsp. nutmeg, ground
- A pinch of salt and black pepper

Directions:

1. In the Foodi, combine the beer with the raisins, cauliflower, salt, pepper and the nutmeg, toss, put the pressure lid on and cook on High for 3 minutes
2. Release the pressure fast for 5 minutes, add the cream mixed with the flour, toss everything, set the pot on Sauté mode and cook everything for 5 minutes more
3. In a bowl mix the bread crumbs with the cheese, stir and sprinkle this over the cauliflower mix.
4. Cover the pot, set it on Air Crisp mode and cook at 390 °F for 10 minutes. Divide everything between plates and serve as a side dish

Garlic Mushrooms

Prep + Cooking Time: 30 minutes, Servings: 4

Ingredients:

- 1 lb. brown mushrooms, halved
- 1 tbsp. garlic; minced.
- 1 tbsp. lime juice
- 1 tbsp. chives; chopped.
- 2 tbsp. olive oil
- Salt and black pepper to the taste

Directions:

1. Set the Foodi on Sauté mode, add the oil and heat it up. Add the garlic and the mushrooms, toss and sauté for 5 minutes
2. Add the lime juice as well, set the machine on Baking mode and cook at 380 °F for 15 minutes. Add the chives, toss, divide everything between plates and serve as a side dish.

Sweet Potato And Mayo

Prep + Cooking Time: 30 minutes, Servings: 2

Ingredients:

- 2 sweet potatoes, peeled and cut into wedges
- 4 tbsp. mayonnaise
- 2 tbsp. olive oil
- ½ tsp. curry powder
- ¼ tsp. coriander, ground
- ½ tsp. cumin, ground
- A pinch of ginger powder
- Salt and black pepper to the taste

Directions:

1. In your Foodi's Air Crisp basket, mix sweet potato wedges with salt, pepper, coriander, curry powder and the oil and toss well
2. Put the basket in the machine, set it on Air Crisp mode and cook the potatoes at 380 °F for 20 minutes shaking the pot halfway. Transfer the potatoes to a bowl, add rest of the ingredients, toss and serve as a side dish

Yummy Eggplant

Prep + Cooking Time: 25 minutes, Servings: 4

Ingredients:

- 4 eggplants, cut into cubes
- 1 red onion; chopped.
- 1 tbsp. smoked paprika
- 1 tbsp. olive oil
- Salt and black pepper to the taste

Directions:

1. Set the Foodi on Sauté mode, add the oil and heat it up. Add the eggplants and all the other ingredients, toss, put the pressure lid on and cook on High for 15 minutes
2. Release the pressure naturally for 10 minutes, divide the mix between plates and serve as a side dish.

Buttery Brussels Sprouts

Prep + Cooking Time: 30 minutes, Servings: 8

Ingredients:

- 3 lbs. Brussels sprouts, trimmed
- 1 lb. bacon; chopped.
- 1 yellow onion; chopped.

- 2 cups heavy cream
- 4 tbsp. butter, melted
- 1 tsp. olive oil
- Salt and black pepper to the taste

Directions:

1. Put the Brussels sprouts in your Foodi's Air Crisp basket and put the basket in the machine
2. Set it on Air Crisp and cook at 370 °F for 10 minutes. Clean the Foodi and put the sprouts in a bowl. Set the machine on Sauté mode, add the oil and the butter and heat it up
3. Return the Sprouts to the pot, also add the bacon and the onion, stir and cook for 5 more minutes. Add the cream, toss, cook or another 5 minutes, divide between plates and as a side dish.

Asian Style Chickpeas

Prep + Cooking Time: 30 minutes, Servings: 4

Ingredients:

- 30 oz. canned chickpeas; drained.
- 2 tbsp. olive oil
- 2 tsp. garam masala
- ¼ tsp. mustard powder
- ½ tsp. garlic powder
- 1 tsp. sweet paprika
- A pinch of salt and black pepper

Directions:

1. In a bowl combine all the ingredients and toss them well. Set the Ninja Foodi on Sauté mode, heat it up for 3 minutes and add the chickpeas and sauté them for 6 minutes
2. Transfer them to the Foodi's basket, place the basket in the pot, set it on Air Crisp and cook at 400 °F for 15 minutes. Divide the chickpeas between plates and serve as a side dish

Bacon and Brussels Sprouts

Prep + Cooking Time: 25 minutes, Servings: 4

Ingredients:

- 1 lb. Brussels sprouts, halved
- 4 bacon strips, cooked and chopped
- 1 tbsp. olive oil
- 2 tsp. garlic powder
- A pinch of salt and black pepper

Directions:

1. In a bowl combine all the ingredients except the bacon and toss. Put the Brussels sprouts in the machine's basket, place the basket inside, set the Foodi on Air Crisp and cook at 390 °F for 20 minutes
2. Divide the Brussels sprouts between plates, sprinkle the bacon on top and serve.

Sweet Potato Mash

Prep + Cooking Time: 25 minutes, Servings: 4

Ingredients:

- 1 ½ lbs. sweet potatoes, peeled and cubed
- 1 cup chicken stock
- 1 tbsp. honey
- 1 tbsp. butter, soft
- Salt and black pepper to the taste

Directions:

1. In your Foodi, mix the sweet potatoes with the stock, salt and pepper, put the pressure lid on and cook on High for 15 minutes. Release the pressure naturally for 10 minutes
2. Mash the potatoes, add the butter and the honey, whisk well, divide between plates and serve as a side dish.

Oregano Potatoes

Prep + Cooking Time: 35 minutes, Servings: 2

Ingredients:

- 4 gold potatoes, cut into wedges
- 4 garlic cloves; minced.
- ½ cup water
- 2 tbsp. olive oil
- 1 tbsp. oregano; chopped.
- Juice of 1 lemon
- A pinch of salt and black pepper

Directions:

1. Put the water in the Foodi machine, add the basket and put the potatoes in it. Put the pressure lid on, set the pot on Low and cook for 4 minutes
2. Release the pressure naturally for 10 minutes, drain the potatoes and put them in a bowl. Clean the pot, set it on Sauté mode, add the oil and heat it up
3. Add the potatoes and the rest of the ingredients, toss, set the machine on Roast and cook at 400 °F for 20 minutes. Divide the potatoes between plates and serve.

Carrot Puree

Prep + Cooking Time: 25 minutes, Servings: 4

Ingredients:

- 1 lb. carrots, peeled and halved
- 1 yellow onion; chopped.
- ½ cup chicken stock
- ¼ cup heavy cream
- Salt and black pepper to the taste

Directions:

1. In your Foodi, combine all the ingredients except the cream, put the pressure lid on and cook on High for 15 minutes. Release the pressure naturally for 10 minutes
2. Mash everything well, add the cream, whisk really well, divide between plates and serve as a side dish.

Baked Mushrooms

Prep + Cooking Time: 25 minutes, Servings: 4

Ingredients:

- 1 lb. white mushrooms, halved
- 1 tbsp. oregano; chopped.
- 2 tbsp. mozzarella cheese; grated.
- 2 tbsp. olive oil
- 1 tbsp. parsley; chopped.
- 1 tbsp. rosemary; chopped.
- Salt and black pepper to the taste

Directions:

1. Set the Foodi on sauté mode, add the oil, heat it up and then combine all the ingredients except the cheese.
2. Sprinkle the cheese on top, set the machine on Baking mode and cook the mushrooms at 380 °F for 15 minutes. Divide the mushrooms between plates and serve as a side dish

Roasted Potatoes

Prep + Cooking Time: 35 minutes, Servings: 4

Ingredients:

- 1 lb. baby potatoes, halved
- ½ cup parsley; chopped.
- ½ cup mayonnaise
- 2 tbsp. tomato paste
- 2 tbsp. olive oil
- 1 tbsp. smoked paprika
- 1 tbsp. garlic powder
- 2 tbsp. white wine vinegar

- 3 tsp. hot paprika
- A pinch of salt and black pepper

Directions:

1. In a bowl combine the potatoes with the paprika, oil, smoked paprika, garlic powder, salt and pepper and toss. Put the potatoes in the basket and place the basket in the Foodi
2. Set the machine on Air Crisp, cook the potatoes for 25 minutes at 360 °F, transfer them to a bowl, mix with the tomato paste, mayo, vinegar and the parsley, toss and serve as a side dish.

Cauliflower Risotto

Prep + Cooking Time: 32 minutes, Servings: 4

Ingredients:

- 1 cauliflower head, riced
- 15 oz. water chestnuts; drained.
- 1 egg; whisked.
- 1 tbsp. ginger; grated.
- 1 tbsp. lemon juice
- 2 tbsp. olive oil
- 4 tbsp. soy sauce
- 3 garlic cloves; minced.

Directions:

1. Set the Foodi on Sauté mode, add the oil and heat it up. Add the garlic and the cauliflower rice, toss and cook for 2-3 minutes
2. Add the soy sauce, chestnuts and the ginger, toss, put the pressure lid on and cook on High for 15 minutes.
3. Release the pressure fast for 5 minutes, set the machine on Sauté mode again, add the egg, stir well and cook for 2 more minutes. Divide between plates and serve as a side dish.

Paprika Beets

Prep + Cooking Time: 45 minutes, Servings: 4

Ingredients:

- 2 lbs. small beets, trimmed and halved
- 1 tbsp. olive oil
- 4 tbsp. sweet paprika

Directions:

1. In a bowl combine all the ingredients and toss them. Put the beets in your Air Crisp basket and put the basket in the Foodi
2. Set on Air Crisp and cook the beets at 380 °F for 35 minutes. Divide the beets between plates and serve as a side dish.

Creamy Artichokes

Prep + Cooking Time: 30 minutes, Servings: 4

Ingredients:

- 15 oz. canned artichoke hearts, roughly
- 1 ½ tbsp. thyme; chopped.
- 2 garlic cloves; minced.
- 1 yellow onion; chopped.
- 1 cup heavy cream
- 1 tbsp. olive oil
- 1 tbsp. parmesan; grated.
- Salt and black pepper to the taste

Directions:

1. Set the Foodi on Sauté mode, add the oil, heat it up, add the onion and the garlic, stir and sauté for 5 minutes. Add all the other ingredients except the thyme and the parmesan, toss, set the machine on Baking mode and cook at 370 °F for 15 minutes
2. Sprinkle the parmesan and the thyme, bake the artichokes mix for 5 more minutes, divide everything between plates and serve.

Broccoli Mash

Prep + Cooking Time: 26 minutes, Servings: 4

Ingredients:

- 1 broccoli head, florets separated and steamed
- ½ cups veggie stock
- ½ tsp. turmeric powder
- 1 tbsp. olive oil
- 1 tbsp. chives; chopped.
- 1 tbsp. butter, melted
- Salt and black pepper to the taste

Directions:

1. Set the Foodi on Sauté mode, add the oil, heat it up, add the broccoli florets and cook them for 4 minutes. Add all the other ingredients except the butter and the chives, put the pressure lid on and cook on High for 12 minutes
2. Release the pressure naturally for 10 minutes, mash the broccoli, add the butter and the chives, whisk everything well, divide between plates and serve.

Cumin Green Beans

Prep + Cooking Time: 20 minutes, Servings: 6

Ingredients:

- 1 lb. green beans, trimmed
- 2 garlic cloves; minced.
- 1 tbsp. olive oil
- ½ tsp. cumin seeds
- Salt and black pepper to the taste

Directions:

1. In a bowl combine all the ingredients and toss well. Put the green beans in the Air Crisp basket and put the basket in the Foodi
2. Set the machine on Air Crisp, cook the green beans at 370 °F for 15 minutes, divide between plates and serve as a side dish.

Lemony Carrots

Prep + Cooking Time: 25 minutes, Servings: 2

Ingredients:

- 1 lb. baby carrots, trimmed
- 2 tsp. olive oil
- 2 tsp. sweet paprika
- Juice of 2 lemons
- Salt and black pepper to the taste

Directions:

1. In a bowl combine all the ingredients and toss them well. Put the carrots in the Air Crisp basket and place it in the Foodi
2. Set the machine on Air Crisp, cook at 400 °F for 15 minutes, divide between plates and serve as a side dish.

Creamy Mushrooms

Prep + Cooking Time: 32 minutes, Servings: 4

Ingredients:

- 8 oz. mushrooms, sliced
- 4 oz. heavy cream
- 2 garlic cloves; minced.
- 1 yellow onion; chopped.
- 1 tbsp. olive oil
- 2 tbsp. parmesan; grated.
- 1 tbsp. parsley; chopped.

Directions:

1. Set the Foodi on Sauté mode, add the oil, heat it up, add the onion and the garlic, stir and cook for 2-3 minutes. Add the mushrooms, salt, pepper and the cream, toss, put the pressure lid on and cook on High for 20 minutes
2. Release the pressure naturally for 10 minutes, add the parmesan and the parsley, toss, divide everything between plates and serve

Carrot Fries

Prep + Cooking Time: 25 minutes, Servings: 4

Ingredients:

- 4 mixed carrots cut into sticks
- 2 garlic cloves; minced.
- 2 tbsp. rosemary; chopped.
- 2 tbsp. olive oil
- Salt and black pepper to the taste

Directions:

1. In a bowl mix all the ingredients and toss them. Put the carrots in the Air Crisp basket and put the basket in the Foodi
2. Set the machine on Air Crisp and cook the fries at 380 °F for 15 minutes. Divide the carrot fries between plates and serve as a side dish.

Chapter 10 Snack & Appetizer Recipes

Creamy Mushroom Dip

Prep + Cooking Time: 35 minutes, Servings: 6

Ingredients:

- 20 oz. cremini mushrooms; chopped.
- 10 oz. Portobello mushrooms; chopped.
- 1 cup chicken stock
- ¼ cup coconut cream
- 1 oz. parmesan cheese; grated.
- ¼ cup olive oil
- 3 garlic cloves; minced.
- 1 yellow onion; chopped.
- 1 tbsp. thyme; chopped.
- 1 tbsp. cilantro; chopped.
- Salt and black pepper to the taste

Directions:

1. Set the Foodi on Sauté mode, add the oil, heat it up, add the onion and the garlic, stir and cook for 5 minutes.
2. Add the rest of the ingredients, toss, put the pressure lid on and cook on High for 20 minutes. Release the pressure naturally for 10 minutes, divide into bowls and serve as a party dip

Cheese Dip

Prep + Cooking Time: 15 minutes, Servings: 8

Ingredients:

- ½ cup pepperoncini peppers; chopped.
- ½ cup sour cream
- 1 ½ cup feta cheese, shredded
- 1 tbsp. olive oil
- 1 tbsp. oregano leaves; minced.
- 1 tbsp. lemon juice
- 1 tsp. Tabasco sauce
- A pinch of salt and black pepper

Directions:

1. In your Foodi's baking dish, combine all the ingredients and toss well. Put the reversible rack in the Foodi, add the baking dish inside, set the machine on Baking mode and cook at 400 °F for 5 minutes
2. Stir the dip one more time, divide it into bowls and serve as a party snack.

Basil Crackers

Prep + Cooking Time: 22 minutes, Servings: 6

Ingredients:

- 1 garlic clove; minced.
- 1 ¼ cups white flour
- ½ tsp. baking powder
- 4 tbsp. butter, melted
- 4 tbsp. basil; minced.
- Salt and black pepper to the taste

Directions:

1. In a bowl mix all the ingredients and stir well until you obtain a dough. Roll the dough on a working surface and cut into medium crackers
2. Arrange all the crackers in the Air Crisp basket and put the basket in the Foodi machine. Grease the crackers with the cooking spray, set the machine on Air Crisp and cook the crackers at 390 °F for 12 minutes. Serve them as a snack.

Colored Pico De Gallo

Prep + Cooking Time: 15 minutes, Servings: 4

Ingredients:

- 1 yellow onion; chopped.
- 4 tomatoes; cubed.
- ¼ cup cilantro; chopped.
- 2 tbsp. lime juice
- A pinch of salt and black pepper

Directions:

1. Put all the ingredients in the Foodi, put the pressure lid on and cook on Low for 5 minutes. Release the pressure naturally for 10 minutes, divide the mix into bowls and serve

Different Hummus

Prep + Cooking Time: 30 minutes, Servings: 6

Ingredients:

- 4 garlic cloves; minced.
- ½ cup veggie stock
- ¼ cup lemon juice
- 2 cups carrots; chopped.
- ¼ cup olive oil
- 1 cup canned chickpeas; drained.

- A pinch of salt and black pepper
- 1 tsp. sweet paprika

Directions:

1. In a bowl mix the carrots with the oil, salt and pepper, toss and leave aside for 10 minutes.
2. Put the carrots in the Air Crisp basket and put the basket in the Foodi
3. Set the machine on Baking mode and cook at 400 °F for 20 minutes. In a blender, mix roasted carrots with all the other ingredients, pulse well, divide into bowls and serve as a snack

Hot Spread

Prep + Cooking Time: 20 minutes, Servings: 4

Ingredients:

- 8 red chilies, dried, seedless and chopped
- ¼ cup veggie stock
- 2 garlic cloves; minced.
- 2 tbsp. apple cider vinegar
- 1 tsp. sugar
- ½ tsp. oregano; chopped.
- Salt and black pepper to the taste

Directions:

1. In your Foodi, combine all the ingredients, toss, put the pressure lid on and cook on High for 10 minutes. Release the pressure naturally for 10 minutes, blend everything using an immersion blender, divide into bowls and serve

Turkey Meatballs

Prep + Cooking Time: 30 minutes, Servings: 6

Ingredients:

- 1 small yellow onion; chopped.
- ¼ cup parmesan; grated.
- ½ cup turkey meat, ground
- 1 egg; whisked.
- 2 garlic cloves; minced.
- 1 tbsp. tomato paste
- 2 tbsp. bread crumbs
- 2 tbsp. parsley; chopped.
- 2 cup marinara sauce
- Cooking spray
- A pinch of salt and black pepper

Directions:

1. In a bowl combine all the ingredients except the cooking spray and the marinara sauce, stir well and shape medium meatballs out of this mix
2. Set the Foodi on Sauté mode, grease with cooking spray and heat it up. Add the meatballs, toss and brown for 3-4 minutes
3. Add the marinara sauce, toss gently, put the pressure lid on and cook on High for 15 minutes. Release the pressure naturally for 10 minutes, divide the meatballs into bowls and serve.

Basil Cream Cheese Dip

Prep + Cooking Time: 12 minutes, Servings: 4

Ingredients:

- 10 kalamata olives, pitted and minced
- 2 oz. bacon, cooked and crumbled
- 4 oz. cream cheese
- 1 tbsp. basil; chopped.
- 2 tbsp. basil pesto
- Salt and black pepper to the taste

Directions:

1. In your Foodi's baking pan, combine all the ingredients and stir well. Put the reversible rack in the Foodi, put the pan in the machine, set it on Baking mode and cook at 360 °F for 8 minutes. Divide the dip into bowls and serve

Broccoli Dip

Prep + Cooking Time: 22 minutes, Servings: 4

Ingredients:

- 1 broccoli head, florets separated
- 1 yellow onion; chopped.
- ½ cup veggie stock
- 1 bunch mint; chopped.
- 2 garlic cloves; minced.
- 1 tbsp. olive oil
- Salt and white pepper to the taste

Directions:

1. Set the Foodi on Sauté mode, add the oil, heat it up, add the onion and the garlic, stir and cook for 2-3 minutes. Add the rest of the ingredients, toss, put the pressure lid on and cook on High for 10 minutes
2. Release the pressure naturally for 10 minutes, blend everything with an immersion blender, divide into bowls and serve.

Wheat Crackers

Prep + Cooking Time: 25 minutes, Servings: 6

Ingredients:

- ½ cup whole wheat flour
- 1/3 cup water
- ½ cup white flour
- 2 tbsp. butter
- 1 tsp. Italian seasoning
- A pinch of salt and black pepper

Directions:

1. In a bowl combine all the ingredients and stir well until you obtain a dough. Roll the dough on a floured working surface and cut into medium squares. Arrange all squares in the Foodi's basket
2. Place the basket in the Ninja Foodi, set the machine on Air Crisp mode and cook at 400 °F for 15 minutes. Serve the crackers cold as a snack.

Balsamic Tomato Salsa

Prep + Cooking Time: 25 minutes, Servings: 6

Ingredients:

- 2 lbs. tomatoes, roughly cubed
- 3 garlic cloves; minced.
- 2 spring onions; chopped.
- 1 cup balsamic vinegar
- 1 tbsp. ginger; grated.
- 1 tsp. sweet paprika
- 1 tsp. chili powder
- ¾ tsp. cinnamon powder
- ½ tsp. coriander, ground

Directions:

1. In your Foodi, combine all the ingredients, put the pressure lid on and cook on High for 15 minutes. Release the pressure naturally for 10 minutes, divide into bowls and serve cold.

Honey Tomato Dip

Prep + Cooking Time: 22 minutes, Servings: 4

Ingredients:

- 1 yellow onion; chopped.
- 2 garlic cloves; minced.
- 1 cup tomato puree

- 1 tbsp. olive oil
- 4 tbsp. white vinegar
- 4 tbsp. honey
- 1 tsp. Tabasco sauce
- Salt and black pepper to the taste

Directions:

1. In your Foodi machine, combine all the ingredients, toss, put the pressure lid on, set on High and cook for 12 minutes. Release the pressure naturally for 10 minutes, stir the mix again, divide into bowls and serve

Tofu Bites

Prep + Cooking Time: 30 minutes, Servings: 4

Ingredients:

- 12 oz. tofu; cubed.
- 1 tbsp. basil pesto
- 2 tbsp. soy sauce
- 1 tsp. hot paprika
- 2 tsp. olive oil

Directions:

1. In a bowl mix all the ingredients and toss well. Put the tofu bites in the Air Crisp basket, put the basket in the Foodi, set the machine on Air Crisp and cook at 350 °F for 20 minutes. Divide the tofu bites into bowls and serve as a snack

Tofu Dip

Prep + Cooking Time: 20 minutes, Servings: 10

Ingredients:

- 4 oz. cream cheese, soft
- 1 yellow onion; chopped.
- 1 tbsp. olive oil
- 3 tbsp. white vinegar
- 1/3 cup sour cream
- ½ cup firm tofu
- A pinch of salt and black pepper

Directions:

1. In your Foodi, combine all the ingredients, put the pressure lid on, set the machine on High and cook for 10 minutes. Release the pressure naturally for 10 minutes, blend everything with an immersion blender, divide into bowls and serve

Crab Sticks

Prep + Cooking Time: 20 minutes, Servings: 12

Ingredients:

- 12 crabsticks
- 2 tsp. olive oil
- 1 tbsp. sweet paprika
- Salt and black pepper to the taste

Directions:

1. In a bowl combine all the ingredients and toss. Put the crabsticks in the Air Crisp basket, put the basket in the Foodi, set the machine on Air Crisp and cook the sticks at 350 °F for 15 minutes. Serve as a snack

Mango and Chili Spread

Prep + Cooking Time: 25 minutes, Servings: 4

Ingredients:

- 2 spring onions; chopped.
- 1 ¼ cup sugar
- 1 ¼ apple cider vinegar
- 2 mangos, peeled chopped
- 2 red hot chilies; chopped.
- 1 tbsp. olive oil
- 2 tbsp. ginger; minced.
- ½ tsp. cinnamon powder

Directions:

1. Set the Foodi on Sauté mode, add the oil, heat it up, add the onions, stir and cook for 2 minutes. Add the other ingredients, put the pressure lid on and cook on High for 12 minutes
2. Release the pressure naturally for 10 minutes, blend everything using an immersion blender, divide into bowls and serve.

Cheese Sticks

Prep + Cooking Time: 20 minutes, Servings: 8

Ingredients:

- 2 eggs; whisked.
- 8 mozzarella cheese strings, halved
- Cooking spray
- 1 tbsp. Italian seasoning
- Salt and black pepper to the taste

Directions:

1. Put the whisked eggs in a bowl. Season mozzarella sticks with salt, pepper and Italian seasoning and dredge them in the egg mix
2. Put the sticks in the Air Crisp basket and put the basket in the Foodi machine. Set the Foodi on Air Crisp mode and cook the sticks at 390 °F for 10 minutes. Serve as a snack

Basil And Paprika Crackers

Prep + Cooking Time: 30 minutes, Servings: 6

Ingredients:

- 1 bunch basil; chopped.
- 4 garlic cloves; minced.
- 1/3 cup water
- 2 cups white flour
- 1 tbsp. sweet paprika
- 2 tbsp. butter, melted

Directions:

1. In a bowl combine all the ingredients and stir well until you obtain a dough. Roll the dough on a floured working surface and cut into medium squares
2. Put the crackers in the Air Crisp basket and put the basket in the Foodi. Set the machine on Air Crisp mode and cook the crackers at 380 °F for 20 minutes. Serve as a snack

Carrot Chips

Prep + Cooking Time: 35 minutes, Servings: 4

Ingredients:

- 4 carrots, thinly sliced
- 1 tsp. olive oil
- ½ tsp. chaat masala
- Salt and black pepper to the taste

Directions:

1. In a bowl mix all the ingredients and toss well. Put the Air Crisp basket in the Foodi, put the chips in the basket, set the machine on Air Crisp and cook at 370 °F for 25 minutes. Serve as a snack

Smoked Dip

Prep + Cooking Time: 20 minutes, Servings: 6

Ingredients:

- 12 oz. red peppers; chopped.
- 1 ¼ cups apple cider vinegar
- 1 tbsp. smoked paprika

- 1 tsp. liquid smoke
- Salt and black pepper to the taste

Directions:

1. In your Foodi, combine all the ingredients, put the pressure lid on and cook on High for 8 minutes. Release the pressure naturally for 10 minutes, blend using an immersion blender, divide into bowls and serve.

Cauliflower Spread

Prep + Cooking Time: 25 minutes, Servings: 6

Ingredients:

- 1 lb. cauliflower florets
- 8 garlic cloves; minced.
- 2 cups veggie stock
- 2 tbsp. butter, melted
- A handful cilantro; chopped.
- Salt and black pepper to the taste

Directions:

1. Set the Foodi on Sauté mode, add the butter, heat it up, add the garlic, stir and cook for 3 minutes. Add the rest of the ingredients, toss, put the pressure lid on and cook on High for 12 minutes
2. Release the pressure naturally for 10 minutes, blend everything using an immersion blender, divide into bowls and serve.

Sweet Potato Chips

Prep + Cooking Time: 25 minutes, Servings: 4

Ingredients:

- 4 sweet potatoes, thinly sliced
- 1 tbsp. olive oil
- Salt and black pepper to the taste

Directions:

1. In a bowl combine all the ingredients and toss. Put the chips in the Air Crisp basket and put the basket in the Foodi. Set the machine on Air Crisp and cook the chips at 400 °F for 15 minutes, flipping them halfway. Serve as a snack

Beets Spread

Prep + Cooking Time: 30 minutes, Servings: 6

Ingredients:

- 6 small beets; grated.
- ½ cup yogurt
- 3 tbsp. lemon juice
- 1 tsp. garlic powder
- Salt and black pepper to the taste

Directions:

1. In your Foodi's baking pan, combine all the ingredients and stir well. Put the reversible rack in the Foodi, put the baking pan inside, set the machine on Baking mode and cook at 360 °F for 20 minutes. Serve as an appetizer

Balsamic Parsnip Sticks

Prep + Cooking Time: 40 minutes, Servings: 6

Ingredients:

- 1 lb. parsnips, thinly cut into sticks
- 2 tbsp. balsamic vinegar
- 2 tbsp. olive oil
- Salt and black pepper to the taste

Directions:

1. In a bowl mix all the ingredients and toss well. Put the sticks in your Foodi's basket, put the basket in the machine, set it on Air Crisp mode and cook at 370 °F for 30 minutes. Serve as a snack

Celery Spread

Prep + Cooking Time: 25 minutes, Servings: 4

Ingredients:

- 1 ½ cups veggie stock
- 1/3 cup coconut cream
- 3 cups celery root; chopped.
- 2 garlic cloves; minced.
- 1 tbsp. white wine vinegar
- 1 tbsp. olive oil
- Salt and black pepper to the taste

Directions:

1. In your Foodi, combine all the ingredients, toss, put the pressure lid on and cook on High for 15 minutes. Release the pressure naturally for 10 minutes, blend using an immersion blender, divide into bowls and serve

Crusted Turkey Bites

Prep + Cooking Time: 25 minutes, Servings: 4

Ingredients:

- 1 lb. turkey breast, skinless, boneless and cubed
- 1 egg; whisked.
- 1 cup white flour
- 1 cup bread crumbs
- ½ tbsp. olive oil
- Salt and black pepper to the taste

Directions:

1. In a bowl mix the flour with salt and pepper and stir. Put the egg in another bowl and the breadcrumbs in a third one
2. Dredge the turkey cubes in flour, egg and bread crumbs and place them in your Air Crisp basket. Put the basket in the Foodi, set the machine on Air Crisp and cook at 400 °F for 15 minutes. Serve the turkey bites as a snack.

Stuffed Mushrooms

Prep + Cooking Time: 25 minutes, Servings: 12

Ingredients:

- 16 oz. canned garbanzo beans; drained.
- 40 mushroom caps
- 1 yellow onion; chopped.
- 2 tbsp. white flour
- 1 tbsp. lemon juice
- 1 tbsp. panko bread crumbs
- ½ tsp. cumin, ground
- ½ tsp. coriander, ground
- A pinch of salt and black pepper

Directions:

1. In a bowl combine all the ingredients except the bread crumbs and the mushroom caps and stir well. Stuff the mushrooms with this mix and sprinkle the panko bread crumbs all over
2. Arrange all the mushrooms in your Air Crisp basket and put the basket in the Foodi machine
3. Set the Ninja Foodi on Air Crisp and cook the mushrooms at 375 °F for 15 minutes. Arrange the mushroom caps on a platter and serve.

Crab Wraps

Prep + Cooking Time: 25 minutes, Servings: 12

Ingredients:

- 12 oz. canned crab meat; drained.
- 16 oz. cream cheese, soft
- 12 oz. wonton wrappers
- ¼ cup mayonnaise
- Zest of ½ lemon
- A pinch of salt and black pepper

Directions:

1. In a bowl combine the crab with the lemon zest, cream cheese, mayo, salt and pepper and stir well. Divide this mix on each wonton wrap, fold and seal the wraps and put them all in the Air Crisp basket
2. Put the basket in the Foodi, set the machine on Air Crisp and cook at 390 °F for 15 minutes. Serve the wraps as an appetizer

Cheese Dip

Prep + Cooking Time: 15 minutes, Servings: 4

Ingredients:

- 2 cups Mexican cheese, cut into chunks
- ¼ cup canned tomatoes; chopped.
- 1 cup bacon, cooked and chopped
- 4 tbsp. chicken stock

Directions:

1. In your Foodi's baking pan, combine all the ingredients. Put the reversible rack in the Foodi, put the baking pan inside, set the machine on Baking mode and cook at 380 °F for 12 minutes. Stir well, divide into bowls and serve as a party dip

Stuffed Peppers

Prep + Cooking Time: 15 minutes, Servings: 4

Ingredients:

- 1 lb. feta cheese, crumbled
- 2 yellow bell peppers, halved lengthwise
- 2 tbsp. oregano; chopped.
- 1 tbsp. chives; chopped.
- Salt and black pepper to the taste

Directions:

1. In a bowl mix the cheese with salt, pepper, chives and oregano and stir well. Stuff the pepper halves with the cheese mix, place them in the Air Crisp basket
2. Put the basket in the Foodi machine, set it on Air Crisp mode and cook at 400 °F for 10 minutes. Serve as an appetizer.

Cilantro Carrot Chips

Prep + Cooking Time: 30 minutes, Servings: 4

Ingredients:

- 1 lb. carrots, thinly sliced
- 1 tbsp. cilantro; chopped.
- 2 tsp. olive oil
- Salt and black pepper to the taste

Directions:

1. In a bowl mix all the ingredients except the cilantro and toss
2. Put the Air Crisp basket in the Foodi, put the chips in the basket, set the machine on Air Crisp and cook at 370 °F for 20 minutes. Serve the chips as a snack with the cilantro sprinkled on top.

Red Peppers Dip

Prep + Cooking Time: 15 minutes, Servings: 8

Ingredients:

- 8 oz. jarred roasted red peppers; chopped.
- 1 cup walnuts, toasted
- 1 ½ tbsp. pomegranate molasses
- 2 tbsp. olive oil
- 1 tbsp. sumac
- 2 tbsp. lemon juice
- 2 tbsp. tomato paste
- 1 tbsp. harissa paste
- 1 tsp. cumin, ground
- A pinch of salt and black pepper

Directions:

1. Set the Foodi on Sauté mode, add the oil, heat it up, add roasted peppers, stir and cook for 2 minutes
2. Add all the other ingredients, put the pressure lid on and cook on High for 3 minutes. Release the pressure naturally for 10 minutes, blend the mix with an immersion blender, divide into bowls and serve.

Buttery Lentils

Prep + Cooking Time: 17 minutes, Servings: 4

Ingredients:

- 15 oz. canned lentils; drained. and rinsed
- 1 tsp. sweet paprika
- 2 tbsp. butter, melted

Directions:

1. In a bowl mix all the ingredients and toss well. Put the lentils in the Air Crisp basket, put the basket in the Foodi, set the machine on Air Crisp and cook at 400 °F for 12 minutes. Serve as a snack

Zucchini Bites

Prep + Cooking Time: 25 minutes, Servings: 6

Ingredients:

- 2 garlic cloves; minced.
- 2 big zucchinis; grated.
- ½ cup cilantro; chopped.
- 1 egg; whisked.
- ½ cup white flour
- Cooking spray
- Salt and black pepper to the taste

Directions:

1. In a bowl mix all the ingredients expect the cooking spray, stir well and shape medium balls out of this mix. Put the basket in the Foodi machine, put the zucchini balls in the basket, grease them with cooking spray, set the machine on Air Crisp and cook at 380 °F for 15 minutes. Serve the balls as a snack

Chickpeas Spread

Prep + Cooking Time: 20 minutes, Servings: 10

Ingredients:

- 2 cups canned chickpeas; drained.
- ¼ cup lemon juice
- ¼ cup olive oil
- ¼ cup veggie stock
- 1 garlic clove; minced.
- 1 tsp. cumin, ground
- 2 tbsp. tahini paste
- A pinch of salt and black pepper

Directions:

1. Put the chickpeas, stock, salt and pepper in the Foodi, put the pressure lid on and cook on High for 10 minutes. Release the pressure naturally for 10 minutes
2. Transfer the chickpeas to a blender, add all the other ingredients, pulse well, divide into bowls and serve.

Cumin Chickpeas Bowls

Prep + Cooking Time: 25 minutes, Servings: 4

Ingredients:

- 15 oz. canned chickpeas; drained., rinsed and dried
- 1 tbsp. olive oil
- ½ tsp. cumin, ground
- 1 tsp. smoked paprika
- Salt and black pepper to the taste

Directions:

1. In a bowl mix all the ingredients and toss them well. Put the chickpeas in the Air Crisp basket, put the basket in the Foodi, set the machine on Air Crisp and cook at 400 °F for 15 minutes. Divide into bowls and serve as a snack

Cayenne Carrot Spread

Prep + Cooking Time: 30 minutes, Servings: 6

Ingredients:

- 2 cups carrots; grated..
- 4 tbsp. butter, melted
- ½ tsp. cayenne pepper
- Salt and black pepper to the taste

Directions:

1. In your Foodi, combine all the ingredients, toss, put the pressure lid on and cook on High for 20 minutes. Release the pressure naturally for 10 minutes, blend using an immersion blender, divide into bowls and serve

Basil Zucchini Dip

Prep + Cooking Time: 30 minutes, Servings: 6

Ingredients:

- 2 zucchinis; chopped.
- 8 garlic cloves; minced.
- 1 bunch basil; chopped.
- 1 yellow onion; chopped.

- 1 cup veggie stock
- ¼ cup lime juice
- 8 carrots; chopped.
- 2 tbsp. olive oil
- Salt and black pepper to the taste

Directions:

1. Set the Foodi on Sauté mode, add the oil, heat it up, add the onions, stir and cook for 4 minutes. Add the other ingredients, toss, put the pressure lid on and cook on High for 20 minutes
2. Release the pressure naturally for 10 minutes, blend everything with an immersion blender, divide into bowls and serve.

Tomato Spread

Prep + Cooking Time: 30 minutes, Servings: 4

Ingredients:

- 30 oz. canned tomatoes, crushed
- 3 garlic cloves; minced.
- 1 cup chicken stock
- 2 cups canned chickpeas; drained.
- Salt and black pepper to the taste

Directions:

1. In your Foodi's baking pan, combine all the ingredients and toss well. Put the reversible rack in the Foodi, add the baking pan inside, set the machine on Baking mode and cook everything at 370 °F for 20 minutes
2. Blend the mix with an immersion blender, divide into bowls and serve

Chapter 11 Dessert Recipes

Caramel Pudding

Prep + Cooking Time: 22 minutes, Servings: 6

Ingredients:

- 8 oz. cream cheese, soft
- 3 eggs
- 1/3 cup sugar
- 2 tbsp. caramel syrup
- 2 tbsp. butter, melted

Directions:

1. In your blender, combine all the ingredients, pulse well and divide into 6 ramekins. Put the reversible rack in the Foodi, add the ramekins inside, set the machine on Baking mode and cook at 320 °F for 12 minutes. Leave aside to cool down and serve

Egg Pudding

Prep + Cooking Time: 35 minutes, Servings: 6

Ingredients:

- 6 egg yolks; whisked.
- 2 cups heavy cream
- 6 tbsp. white sugar
- Zest of 1 lemon; grated.

Directions:

1. In a bowl mix all the ingredients, whisk well and divide into 6 ramekins. Put the reversible rack in the Foodi, arrange the ramekins inside, set the machine on Baking mode and cook at 340 °F for 25 minutes. Cool down and serve

Buttery Rolls

Prep + Cooking Time: 2 hours 10 minutes, Servings:8

Ingredients:

- 1 lb. bread dough
- ¼ cup butter, melted
- ¾ cup brown sugar

Directions:

1. Roll the dough on a floured working surface, shape a rectangle and brush with the butter. Sprinkle the sugar all over, roll the dough into a log and cut into 8 pieces

2. Leave the rolls to rise in a warm place for 2 hours. Put the Air Crisp basket in the Foodi and put the rolls in the basket. Set the machine on Air Crisp, cook at 350 °F for 10 minutes Serve warm

Sweet Bread

Prep + Cooking Time: 25 minutes, Servings: 4

Ingredients:

- 8 oz. flour
- 4 oz. milk
- 1 egg
- 2 tbsp. butter
- 2 tbsp. white sugar
- 1 tsp. baking powder

Directions:

1. In a bowl mix all the ingredients and stir well. Transfer the dough to a loaf pan that fits the Foodi. Put the reversible rack in the Foodi and put the loaf pan inside
2. Set the machine on Baking mode and cook at 360 °F for 15 minutes. Slice the sweet bread and serve it warm.

Butter Brownies

Prep + Cooking Time: 35 minutes, Servings: 12

Ingredients:

- 2 eggs
- 2 cups white flour
- 1 cup butter, melted
- ½ cup chocolate chips; chopped.
- 4 tbsp. sugar
- 1 tsp. vanilla extract

Directions:

1. In a bowl mix all the ingredients, whisk well and pour into your Foodi's cake pan. Put the reversible rack in the Foodi, put the cake pan inside, set the machine on Baking mode and cook at 330 °F for 25 minutes. Cool down, slice and serve

Awesome Cake

Prep + Cooking Time: 35 minutes, Servings: 8

Ingredients:

- 15 oz. cake mix
- ½ cup chocolate chips.

- Cooking spray

Directions:

1. In a bowl combine all the ingredients and whisk well. Grease the Foodi's cake pan with cooking spray and pour the cake mix in it
2. Put the reversible rack in the Foodi, add the cake pan inside, set the machine on Baking mode and cook the cake at 350 °F for 25 minutes. Cool the cake down, slice and serve.

Apple Cake

Prep + Cooking Time: 60 minutes, Servings: 4

Ingredients:

- 40 oz. apple flesh
- 14 oz. cake mix
- 8 oz. butter, soft
- 1 tsp. cinnamon powder
- Cooking spray

Directions:

1. Grease your Foodi's cake pan with the cooking spray and layer the apple flesh on the bottom. In a bowl mix the butter with the cooking spray and spread this over the apple mix
2. Sprinkle the cinnamon on top, put the cake pan in the Foodi, set the machine on Baking mode and cook at 360 °F for 50 minutes. Cool the cake down, slice and serve

Chocolate Cream

Prep + Cooking Time: 25 minutes, Servings: 6

Ingredients:

- 12 oz. chocolate chips
- 1 cup heavy cream
- 1 cup sugar
- ½ cup butter, melted

Directions:

1. In a bowl mix all the ingredients, whisk well and divide everything into 6 ramekins. Put the reversible rack in the Foodi, put the ramekins inside, set the machine on Baking mode and cook at 350 °F for 15 minutes. Serve the cream cold

Pumpkin Cake

Prep + Cooking Time: 60 minutes, Servings: 12

Ingredients:

- 14 oz. cake mix
- 2 oz. chocolate chips
- 12 oz. pumpkin puree
- 1 cup cranberries, dried
- 1 tbsp. pumpkin pie spice

Directions:

1. In a bowl combine all the ingredients, stir well and pour into your Foodi's cake pan. Put the reversible rack in the Foodi, add the cake pan inside, set the machine on Baking mode and cook at 350 °F for 50 minutes. Slice the cake and serve

Black Beans Brownies

Prep + Cooking Time: 30 minutes, Servings: 12

Ingredients:

- 4 oz. chocolate; chopped.
- 4 eggs; whisked.
- 1 cup white flour
- ½ cup canned black beans; drained. and blended
- ½ cup butter, melted
- ¼ cup brewed black coffee
- 1 ¼ cups sugar
- 1 tsp. vanilla extract
- Cooking spray

Directions:

1. In a bowl combine all the ingredients except the cooking spray and whisk well. Grease a cake pan with the cooking spray and pour the batter in it
2. Put the reversible rack in the Foodi, add the cake pan inside, set the machine on Baking mode and cook at 350 °F for 20 minutes. Slice the brownies and serve

Cocoa And Orange Pudding

Prep + Cooking Time: 30 minutes, Servings: 4

Ingredients:

- 1 egg
- 2 tbsp. orange juice
- 4 tbsp. white flour
- 1 tbsp. cocoa powder

- 4 tbsp. sugar
- 2 tbsp. coconut oil, melted
- 4 tbsp. milk
- ½ tsp. baking powder
- ½ tsp. lime zest; grated.

Directions:

1. In a bowl mix all the ingredients, stir well and divide into 4 ramekins. Put the reversible rack in the Foodi, put the ramekins inside, set the machine on Baking mode and cook 320 °F for 20 minutes. Serve the pudding warm

Apple Pie

Prep + Cooking Time: 60 minutes, Servings: 8

Ingredients:

- 2 apples, cored, peeled and sliced
- 2 eggs; whisked.
- ¾ cup milk
- 2/3 cup white flour
- 1/3 cup sugar
- Cooking spray
- 2 tbsp. flavored liqueur
- 1 tsp. cinnamon powder

Directions:

1. In a bowl mix the sugar with the cinnamon, flour, eggs, milk and the liqueur and stir well. Grease the Foodi's cake pan with cooking spray and arrange the apples into the pan
2. Pour the batter over the apples and put the pan in the Foodi. Set the machine on Baking mode and cook at 400 °F for 55 minutes. Cool the pie down, slice and serve.

Apples Jam

Prep + Cooking Time: 30 minutes, Servings: 6

Ingredients:

- 1 lb. apples, peeled, cored and chopped
- 2 lbs. sugar
- 2 cups apple juice
- Juice of 2 limes

Directions:

1. In your Foodi, combine all the ingredients, toss, put the pressure lid on and cook on High for 20 minutes. Blend the mix using an immersion blender, divide into cups and serve cold

Pineapple And Yogurt Cake

Prep + Cooking Time: 50 minutes, Servings: 6

Ingredients:

- 5 oz. flour
- 1 egg; whisked.
- ½ cup sugar
- 1/3 cup coconut flakes, shredded
- ¼ cup pineapple juice
- 4 tbsp. vegetable oil
- 3 tbsp. yogurt
- ¾ tsp. baking powder
- ½ tsp. baking soda
- ½ tsp. cinnamon powder
- Cooking spray

Directions:

1. In a bowl mix all the ingredients except the cooking spray and whisk well. Grease the Foodi's cake pan with cooking spray and pour the cake batter inside
2. Put the reversible rack in the Foodi, put the cake pan on the rack, set the machine on baking mode and cook the cake at 320 °F for 40 minutes. Cool down, cut and serve it.

Creamy Orange Cake

Prep + Cooking Time: 40 minutes, Servings: 10

Ingredients:

- 9 oz. white flour
- 2 oz. sugar
- 4 oz. cream cheese
- 6 eggs; whisked.
- 1 orange, peeled and pureed
- 1 tsp. vanilla extract
- 1 tsp. baking powder

Directions:

1. In a food processor, combine all the ingredients, pulse well and spread into the Foodi's cake pan.
2. Put the reversible rack in the Foodi, put the cake pan inside, set the machine on Baking mode and cook at 340 °F for 30 minutes. Cool the cake down, slice and serve

Raisins Pudding

Prep + Cooking Time: 60 minutes, Servings: 4

Ingredients:

- ½ cups cherries, pitted and halved.
- 4 egg yolks
- 1 ½ cups coconut cream
- ¼ cup sugar
- ½ cup chocolate chips
- 1 cup raisins

Directions:

1. In a bowl mix all the ingredients, stir well and pour everything into a ramekin. Put the reversible rack in the Foodi and place the ramekin inside
2. Set the machine on Baking mode, cook the pudding at 310 °F for 50 minutes, cool down and serve.

Cream Cheese Cake

Prep + Cooking Time: 25 minutes, Servings: 10

Ingredients:

- 6 oz. coconut oil, melted
- 3 oz. cocoa powder
- 4 oz. cream cheese, soft
- 6 eggs
- 5 tbsp. sugar
- 2 tsp. vanilla extract
- ½ tsp. baking powder

Directions:

1. In a blender, combine all the ingredients, pulse well and pour this into your Foodi's cake pan. Put the reversible rack in the Foodi machine, add the cake pan inside, set the pot on Baking mode and cook at 320 °F, bake for 15 minutes. Slice and serve

Banana Cupcakes

Prep + Cooking Time: 30 minutes, Servings: 12

Ingredients:

- 14 oz. cake mix
- 3 bananas, peeled and mashed
- Cooking spray

Directions:

1. In a bowl combine all the ingredients and stir well. Grease a cupcake pan with cooking spray and pour the cake mix into the pan
2. Put the reversible rack in the Foodi, put the cupcake pan inside, set the machine on Baking mode and cook at 350 °F for 20 minutes. Serve the cupcakes cold

Dark Chocolate Creamy Pudding

Prep + Cooking Time: 22 minutes, Servings: 4

Ingredients:

- 4 oz. dark chocolate, cut into chunks and melted
- 4 oz. heavy cream

Directions:

1. In 4 ramekins, combine the ingredients and whisk well. Put the reversible rack in the Foodi, put the ramekins inside, set the machine on Baking mode and cook at 300 °F for 12 minutes. Serve cold

Mango Bowls

Prep + Cooking Time: 30 minutes, Servings: 4

Ingredients:

- 4 mangos, peeled and roughly cut into cubes
- ¼ cup brown sugar
- 2 tsp. cinnamon powder
- 4 tbsp. butter, melted

Directions:

1. In your Foodi's baking pan, combine all the ingredients and toss. Put the reversible rack in the Foodi, add the baking pan inside, set the machine on Baking mode and cook at 300 °F for 20 minutes. Divide the mix into bowls and serve

Irish Brownies

Prep + Cooking Time: 35 minutes, Servings: 12

Ingredients:

- 1 cup white flour
- 4 oz. baking chocolate; chopped. and melted
- ½ cup butter, melted
- ½ cup sugar
- ¼ cup Irish cream liqueur
- 2 eggs; whisked.
- ½ tsp. baking powder
- Cooking spray

Directions:

1. In a bowl mix all the ingredients except the cooking spray and stir really well. Grease the Foodi's cake pan with the cooking spray and pour the brownie batter into the pan
2. Set the machine on Baking mode and cook at 350 °F for 25 minutes. Cool the mix down, slice and serve.

Pumpkin Pie

Prep + Cooking Time: 40 minutes, Servings: 8

Ingredients:

- 4 oz. pumpkin flesh; chopped.
- 3 oz. water
- 1 egg; whisked.
- 1 pie crust
- 1 tsp. nutmeg, ground
- 1 tbsp. sugar

Directions:

1. In a blender, combine all the ingredients except the pie crust, pulse well and spread the mix into the pie crust.
2. Put the reversible rack in the Foodi, put the pie into the pot, set it on Baking mode and cook the pie at 360 °F for 30 minutes. Slice and serve warm

White Chocolate Cheesecake

Prep + Cooking Time: 80 minutes, Servings: 8

Ingredients:

- 24 oz. cream cheese, soft
- 12 oz. white chocolate, melted
- 1 ½ cups cookies, crumbled

- ½ cup heavy cream
- 1 cup sugar
- 3 eggs; whisked.
- 4 tbsp. butter, melted
- 1 tbsp. vanilla extract

Directions:

1. In a bowl mix cookie crumbs with the butter, stir, spread this on the bottom of your Foodi's cake pan and freeze for now. In another bowl, mix the other ingredients, whisk well and spread over the crust
2. Put the reversible rack in the Foodi, put the cake pan inside, set the machine on Baking mode and cook at 320 °F for 20 minutes. Cool the cheesecake down and keep in the fridge for 1 hour before serving.

Lime Cake

Prep + Cooking Time: 30 minutes, Servings: 4

Ingredients:

- 1 egg; whisked.
- 4 tbsp. milk
- 4 tbsp. flour
- 4 tbsp. white sugar
- 2 tbsp. butter, melted
- ½ tsp. baking powder
- 1 tsp. lime zest; grated.
- 1 tsp. lime juice
- Cooking spray

Directions:

1. In a bowl mix all the ingredients except the cooking spray, stir well and pour into your Foodi's cake pan after you've greased it with cooking spray
2. Put the reversible rack in the Foodi, put the cake pan inside, set the machine on Baking mode and cook at 320 °F for 20 minutes. Serve the cake right away

Buttery Apples

Prep + Cooking Time: 25 minutes, Servings: 4

Ingredients:

- 4 apples, peeled, cored and halved
- 3 tbsp. butter, melted
- 3 tbsp. sugar

Directions:

1. In the Foodi's baking pan, combine all the ingredients and toss. Put the reversible rack in the Foodi, put the baking pan inside, set the machine on Baking mode and cook at 370 °F for 15 minutes. Serve warm

Blueberries Cake

Prep + Cooking Time: 50 minutes, Servings: 12

Ingredients:

- 1 pint blueberries
- 2 eggs; whisked.
- 1/3 cup brown sugar
- 4 cups water
- 2 cups cake baking mix
- 1 cup Greek yogurt
- 2 tbsp. coconut oil, melted
- 2 tbsp. lemon peel; grated.
- 2 tbsp. lemon juice
- 1 tsp. baking powder
- 1 tsp. vanilla extract
- Cooking spray

Directions:

1. In a bowl combine all the ingredients except the cooking spray and the water and whisk well. Put the water into the Foodi and place the reversible rack in the machine
2. Grease the cake pan with cooking spray and pour the cake batter in it. Put the cake pan in the Foodi, set the machine on Baking mode and cook at 350 °F for 40 minutes. Slice the cake and serve.

Bread Pudding

Prep + Cooking Time: 35 minutes, Servings: 4

Ingredients:

- 4 egg yolks; whisked.
- 2 cups milk
- 1 cup sugar
- 2 cups heavy cream
- 3 cups white bread; cubed.
- ½ tsp. vanilla extract
- 2 tbsp. butter, melted
- Zest of ½ lemon; grated.

Directions:

1. In a bowl mix all the ingredients, whisk well and pour this into the Foodi's baking pan

2. Put the reversible rack in the Foodi, add the baking pan inside, set the machine on Baking mode and cook at 330 °F for 30 minutes. Cool the pudding down and serve

Yogurt Cake

Prep + Cooking Time: 30 minutes, Servings: 6

Ingredients:

- 8 oz. canned pumpkin puree
- 1 egg; whisked.
- ¾ cup sugar
- 1 cup white flour
- 1 cup Greek yogurt
- 1 tsp. baking powder
- Cooking spray

Directions:

1. In a bowl combine all the ingredients except the cooking spray and whisk well. Grease the Foodi's cake pan with cooking spray and pour the batter in it
2. Put the reversible rack in the Foodi, add the cake pan inside, set the machine on Baking mode and cook at 330 °F for 20 minutes. Cool the cake down, slice and serve.

Lime Quinoa Pudding

Prep + Cooking Time: 25 minutes, Servings: 6

Ingredients:

- 1/3 cup quinoa
- 2 cups milk
- ½ cup sugar
- Zest of 1 lime; grated.

Directions:

1. In a ramekin, combine all the ingredients and whisk. Put the reversible rack in the Foodi, put the ramekin inside, set the machine on Baking mode and cook at 320 °F for 15 minutes. Divide into bowls and serve

Carrot Bread

Prep + Cooking Time: 45 minutes, Servings: 6

Ingredients:

- 3 cups carrots; grated.
- 2 eggs; whisked.
- 1 cup sugar
- 2 cups white flour

- 1 stick butter, melted
- 1 tbsp. baking powder
- 1 tbsp. vanilla extract

Directions:

1. In a bowl mix all the ingredients, stir well and pour into a loaf pan that fits the Foodi.
2. Put the reversible rack in the Foodi and put the loaf pan inside. Set the machine on Baking mode and cook at 320 °F for 35 minutes. Slice and serve warm

Zucchini Bread

Prep + Cooking Time: 50 minutes, Servings: 6

Ingredients:

- 2 zucchinis; grated.
- 1 egg
- ¾ cup sugar
- 1/3 cup butter, melted
- 1/3 cup milk
- 1 tsp. vanilla extract
- 1 tsp. baking powder
- 1 ½ cups flour
- ½ tsp. baking soda

Directions:

1. In a bowl mix all the ingredients, stir well and pour into a loaf pan lined with parchment paper.
2. Put the reversible rack in the Foodi and put the loaf pan inside. Set the machine on Baking mode and cook at 320 °F for 40 minutes Cool down, slice and serve it

Cinnamon Pears

Prep + Cooking Time: 25 minutes, Servings: 4

Ingredients:

- 4 pears, cored and cut into wedges
- ¼ cup brown sugar
- 1 tbsp. maple syrup
- 4 tbsp. butter, melted
- 2 tsp. cinnamon powder

Directions:

1. In your Foodi's baking pan, combine all the ingredients and toss. Put the reversible rack into the Foodi, put the baking pan inside, set the machine on Baking mode and cook at 360 °F for 15 minutes. Divide between dessert plates and serve

Apple Bread

Prep + Cooking Time: 50 minutes, Servings: 6

Ingredients:

- 3 apples, peeled and pureed
- 2 eggs; whisked.
- 2 cups white flour
- 1 cup sugar
- 1 stick of butter, melted
- 1 tbsp. baking powder

Directions:

1. In a bowl mix all the ingredients and whisk well. Pour this into a loaf pan that fits the Foodi. Put the reversible rack in the Foodi, put the loaf pan inside, set the machine on Baking mode and cook at 340 °F for 40 minutes. Cool the sweet bread down, slice and serve

Apple Pudding

Prep + Cooking Time: 35 minutes, Servings: 6

Ingredients:

- 4 apples, peeled, cored and pureed
- 1 cup milk
- 1 cup maple syrup
- 2 eggs; whisked.
- 1 tbsp. cornstarch
- 1 tsp. cinnamon powder

Directions:

1. In a bowl mix all the ingredients, whisk and divide into 6 ramekins. Put the reversible rack in the Foodi, put the ramekins inside, set the machine on Baking mode and cook at 340 °F for 25 minutes. Serve the pudding warm.

Easy Cake

Prep + Cooking Time: 50 minutes, Servings: 6

Ingredients:

- 2 eggs; whisked.
- 1 cup ricotta cheese, soft
- ¼ cup walnuts; chopped.
- 1 cup white flour
- ½ cup sugar
- ½ cup cocoa powder
- 3 tbsp. butter, melted

- 2 tsp. baking powder

Directions:

1. In a bowl mix all the ingredients and whisk well. Pour the mix into the Foodi's cake pan and put the pan in the machine on the reversible rack
2. Set the Foodi on Baking mode, cook the cake at 320 °F for 40 minutes, cool down, slice and serve.

Blackberries Cream

Prep + Cooking Time: 25 minutes, Servings: 4

Ingredients:

- 8 oz. cream cheese
- 4 oz. blackberries.
- ½ cup heavy cream
- ½ tbsp. lime juice
- 2 tbsp. water
- ¼ tsp. sugar

Directions:

1. In your blender, mix all the ingredients, pulse well and divide into 4 ramekins. Put the reversible rack in the Foodi, put the ramekins inside, set the machine on Baking mode and cook at 340 °F for 15 minutes. Serve the cream cold

Graham Cheesecake

Prep + Cooking Time: 25 minutes, Servings: 8

Ingredients:

- 1 lb. cream cheese, soft
- 1 cup graham cookies, crumbled
- 2 eggs; whisked.
- 4 tbsp. brown sugar
- 2 tbsp. butter, melted
- ½ tsp. vanilla extract
- Cooking spray

Directions:

1. In a bowl mix the cookies with the butter and press this on the bottom of a cake pan greased with cooking spray. In a bowl mix all the other ingredients, stir well and pour over the graham cookie crust
2. Put the reversible rack in the Foodi, put the cake pan inside, set the machine on Baking mode and cook at 320 °F 15 minutes. Keep the cheesecake in the fridge for a few hours before serving.

Creamy Strawberries

Prep + Cooking Time: 24 minutes, Servings: 6

Ingredients:

- 1 cup strawberries
- ½ cup heavy cream
- ½ cup butter, melted
- 2 eggs; whisked.
- 2 tsp. vanilla extract
- 2 tsp. baking powder
- 5 tbsp. sugar

Directions:

1. In a bowl mix all the ingredients, whisk well and divide into 6 ramekins. Put the reversible rack in the Foodi, put the ramekins inside, set the machine on Baking mode and cook at 320 °F for 12 minutes. Serve the mix cold.

Blueberries Stew

Prep + Cooking Time: 22 minutes, Servings: 4

Ingredients:

- 1 lb. blueberries.
- 30 oz. grape juice
- Juice and zest of 1 lemon

Directions:

1. In your Foodi, combine all the ingredients, put the pressure lid on and cook on High for 12 minutes. Release the pressure naturally for 10 minutes, divide everything into cups and serve

Apple Stew

Prep + Cooking Time: 25 minutes, Servings: 4

Ingredients:

- 4 apples, cored and cut into wedges
- 2 cups orange juice
- 2 and ¼ cups white sugar

Directions:

1. In your Foodi, combine all the ingredients, toss, put the pressure lid on and cook on High for 15 minutes. Release the pressure naturally for 10 minutes, divide the sweet stew into bowls and serve

Cinnamon Apples

Prep + Cooking Time: 25 minutes, Servings: 4

Ingredients:

- 2 apples, cored
- 2 tbsp. sugar
- ½ tsp. cinnamon powder

Directions:

1. Put the pears in your Foodi's basket and put the basket in the pot. Set the machine on Air Crisp mode, cook the apples at 320 °F for 15 minutes and serve them warm

Pear Cake

Prep + Cooking Time: 50 minutes, Servings: 6

Ingredients:

- 2 pears, peeled and chopped
- 1 egg; whisked.
- 1 cup sugar
- 1 ½ cups white flour
- 1/3 cup milk
- 1/3 cup butter, melted
- 1 tsp. vanilla extract
- 1 tsp. baking powder
- Cooking spray

Directions:

1. In a bowl mix all the ingredients except the cooking spray and stir well. Grease the Foodi's cake pan with the cooking spray and pour the cake batter inside
2. Put the reversible rack in the Foodi, add the cake pan inside, set the machine on Baking mode and cook at 340 °F for 40 minutes. Cool the cake down, slice and serve

Tasty Brownies

Prep + Cooking Time: 70 minutes, Servings: 6

Ingredients:

- 6 oz. chocolate chips, melted
- 2 eggs; whisked.
- ¾ cup butter, melted
- ½ cup sugar
- ½ cup brown sugar
- ¼ cup cocoa powder
- ½ cup white flour

- 1 tbsp. water
- 1 tbsp. vanilla extract
- Cooking spray

Directions:

1. In a bowl combine all the ingredients except the cooking spray and stir well. Grease your Foodi's cake pan with the cooking spray and pour the batter into the pan
2. Put the reversible rack in the Foodi, put the cake pan inside, set the machine on Air Crisp and cook at 300 °F for 1 hour. Cool the mix down, cut into medium pieces and serve

Chocolate Cheesecake

Prep + Cooking Time: 30 minutes, Servings: 6

Ingredients:

- 16 oz. cream cheese, soft
- 2 eggs; whisked.
- ½ cup chocolate cookies, crumbled
- ½ cup sugar
- 2 tsp. butter, melted
- ½ tsp. vanilla extract

Directions:

1. Grease the Foodi's cake pan with the butter and spread cookie crumbs on the bottom. In a bowl mix all the other ingredients, whisk well and spread over the crust
2. Put the reversible rack in the Foodi, put the cake pan inside, set the machine on Baking mode, cook at 340 °F for 20 minutes. Cool the cake down and serve cold

Cocoa Cookies

Prep + Cooking Time: 27 minutes, Servings: 4

Ingredients:

- 1 egg
- ¼ cup white flour
- ½ cup cocoa powder
- 1/3 cup sugar
- 8 tbsp. butter, melted
- ½ tsp. baking powder
- ½ tsp. vanilla extract

Directions:

1. In a bowl mix all the ingredients and stir well. Spread this cooking batter into the Foodi's cake pan.

2. Put the reversible rack in the Foodi, put the cake pan inside, set the machine on Baking mode and cook at 320 °F for 17 minutes. Leave the cookie mix to cool down, cut and serve

Ricotta Cake

Prep + Cooking Time: 45 minutes, Servings: 6

Ingredients:

- 2 cups ricotta cheese
- 1 egg; whisked.
- 1 cup white flour
- ¼ cup sugar
- 1 tbsp. lemon juice
- 3 tbsp. butter, melted
- 1 tsp. vanilla extract
- 2 tsp. baking powder

Directions:

1. In a bowl mix all the ingredients, whisk well and pour into the Foodi's cake pan
2. Put the reversible rack in the Foodi, put the cake pan inside, set the machine on Baking mode and cook at 340 °F for 35 minutes. Cool the cake down, slice and serve.

Peach Cake

Prep + Cooking Time: 40 minutes, Servings: 4

Ingredients:

- 8 oz. peaches; chopped.
- 2 oz. butter
- 1 cup white flour
- 1 cup sugar
- 4 eggs; whisked.
- 3 tbsp. maple syrup
- 1 tsp. cinnamon powder
- 3 tsp. baking powder

Directions:

1. In a bowl mix all the ingredients, stir well and pour into the Foodi's cake pan. Put the reversible rack in the Foodi, put the cake pan inside, set the machine on Baking mode and cook mix at 340 °F for 30 minutes. Once done leave the cake to cool down, slice and serve

CPSIA information can be obtained
at www.ICGtesting.com
Printed in the USA
LVHW101710221220
674884LV00014B/699

9 781637 331163